Joe Ehrmann
then and now

Season of Life

A football star, a boy,
a journey to manhood

Jeffrey Marx

Simon & Schuster
NEW YORK · LONDON · TORONTO · SYDNEY

SIMON & SCHUSTER
Rockefeller Center
1230 Avenue of the Americas
New York, NY 10020

For information regarding special discounts for bulk purchases,
please contact Simon & Schuster Special Sales at 1-800-456-6798
or business@simonandschuster.com

"That Guy in the Glass" appears in this book exactly as it was
found on a sign outside the Colts' locker room. A slightly different
(and apparently the original) version of the poem, entitled
"The Guy in the Glass," has been credited to Peter "Dale"
Wimbrow Sr. and can be found at www.theguyintheglass.com.

DESIGNED BY PAUL DIPPOLITO

Manufactured in the United States of America

21 23 25 27 29 30 28 26 24 22

Library of Congress Cataloging-in-Publication Data
Marx, Jeffrey, 1962–
Season of life : a football star, a boy, a journey to manhood / Jeffrey Marx.
p. cm.
1. Ehrmann, Joe. 2. Marx, Jeffrey, 1962– 3. Football coaches—Maryland—
Baltimore—Biography. 4. Gilman School (Baltimore, Md.)—Football.
I. Title
GV939.E45M37 2004
796.332'092—dc22
[B]   2004052493

ISBN 0-7432-6974-8

For Richard Marx, without whom I have no story at all

This book is also dedicated to the memory of Wendy Marx,
my only sister and best friend, my silent hero,
forever my inspiration

Acknowledgments

This book could be written only because an old friend, Joe Ehrmann, welcomed me back into his life. I thank Joe and his wife, Paula, for giving me three wonderful gifts—their time, their kindness, and their trust. Biff and Amy Poggi graciously shared the same trio of offerings with me. I am enormously grateful for the way they opened their doors and their hearts to someone they were just getting to know.

I also want to thank the many good people at Gilman School who always made me feel like I belonged. That includes all the boys on the 2001 football team and their families. It also includes the following coaches and other members of the Gilman community: Buzz Battaglia, Lori Bristow, Sherm Bristow, Frank Culotta, Johnnie Foreman, Timothy Holley, Keith Kormanik, Josh Mason, Jon McGill, Ray Mills, David Payne, Nick Pitruzzella, Brendan Schenning, Carol Schuch, Faye and Elias Shaya, Edward Trusty, Rob White, and Stan White.

Working on a book—at least for this struggling writer—requires much support from an army of friends and family. I never would have made it through this process without the love and understanding of Leslie Herpin ("Po" to me). Thank you, Po, for being here whenever I needed you most. I also thank the following for always allowing me to go on and on with my endless stream of book talk: Virginia Anderson, Dale Brown, John and Lee Carroll, Tom Connolly, Frank Deford, Joe Douglas, E. David Ellington and Wendy

Marx Ellington, Dan Forstein and Peggy Marx, Rusty Gorman, Lauren Hochman, Bert Jones, Greg Katz, Carl Lewis, Toni and Renate Linhart, Mitch Loveman, Jim and Patti Marx, Richard and Leslie Marx, Harry Merritt, Peter Ripka, Dane and Daniella Strother, Bret Talbot, Merv Wampold, Mike Woodrow, and Michael and Becky York.

Finally, I want to offer my deep thanks to the people who have contributed most directly—with advice, edits, design, and kindness—to the preparation of this book: Bob Bender, Flip Brophy, Carl Cannon, Tina Croley, Emily Loose, Trina Lucido, Michael O'Shea, and Ray Walker. An extra-large bundle of thanks goes to my editor, Carl Cannon, who has now managed to red-ink his way through all four of my books. Thank you, as always, Carl, for saving me from myself whenever I was wise enough to let you.

Season
of Life

Chapter One

YOUNG FACES USUALLY FILLED WITH WARMTH AND wonder were now taut with anticipation and purpose. Eyes were lasers. Hearts were pounding. It was nothing unusual for the explosive combination of testosterone and youth to unleash a wild display of emotions in the minutes leading up to the start of a high school football game—and this was no ordinary game for the boys of Gilman School. This was the season opener, being played in front of three thousand screaming fans, and it featured the type of marquee matchup typically saved for a championship contest at the end of a year. Gilman was the top-ranked high school team in all of Maryland. Its opponent was second-ranked DeMatha.

The Gilman boys were decked out in crisp white jerseys and plain gray helmets turned shiny silver by the stadium lights. They were not only schoolboys now. They were also the mighty Greyhounds. The Greyhounds paced. They gnashed teeth. They pounded one another on the shoulder pads.

"Pancakes," one of the senior captains growled, meaning he wanted to see opponents knocked flat on the ground. "I'm looking for pancakes."

A sophomore linebacker, normally a very polite and respectful fifteen-year-old, spoke from behind an overdone smearing of eye black that transformed his face into something of a Halloween mask: "They don't want to ask us any questions, 'cause I promise you, we're gonna give 'em some answers."

"Time to get busy!" another boy shouted toward the Friday night sky.

Joe Ehrmann had already seen and heard it all too many times for any of this to affect him a whole lot. He'd seen and heard it as an All-American defensive lineman—big mountain of a man, six-foot-four, 260 well-packed pounds—at Syracuse University. He'd seen and heard it throughout his thirteen years as a professional football player, most of them as a star with the Baltimore Colts, one of the most storied franchises in the history of the National Football League. He'd seen and heard it during five years of coaching at Gilman. At the age of fifty-two, Joe was no longer fazed by the specific circumstances of any single game. No victory or defeat, no matter how glorious or excruciating for his team, would ever eclipse the only reason he was there. What do points on a scoreboard have to do with teaching boys how to be men of substance and impact? Nothing. And that explained the absolute calmness with which Joe now walked toward his huddled team for final comments just before the start of the 2001 season. Actually, Joe did not walk so much as he shuffled, gingerly calculating his steps, which sometimes moved him side to side almost as much as they advanced him. Joe was prematurely hobbled by the residue of countless full-body crashes on football fields across America, his right side held together by an artificial hip, his left side permanently hampered by long-ago surgery that left him with almost no flexibility in either his ankle or his foot.

Joe's brown eyes peered through gold-rimmed glasses that conspired with his white hair—with his closely trimmed white beard and mustache as well—to make him look more like a college professor than a jock. He reached into a pocket of his khaki pants for his ever-present tin of peppermint Altoids. That was the only thing Joe carried onto the field. He did not need a clipboard because he coached from the heart. He did not need a whistle because his players automatically fell silent when he stood before them.

"This is one of the greatest experiences of your young lives," Joe told the boys. "So let's make sure you're having fun, all right? You've been doing a lot of work the last few weeks to get ready for this. Now's the time you can let it all hang out. Let's get after them. We're *gonna* get after 'em. But let's make sure we're having fun."

Other coaches spoke. Then Joe initiated his standard question-and-answer sequence.

"What is our job as coaches?" he asked.

"To love us," the boys yelled back in unison.

"What is *your* job?" Joe shot back.

"To love each other," the boys responded.

The words were spoken with the familiarity of a mantra, the commitment of an oath, the enthusiasm of a pep rally.

This was football?

What was going on here? How in the world had I, an out-of-town writer in the final year of my thirties, become so wrapped up in it all? And how could I possibly have foreseen the gift of my own transformative experience that would soon be coming? How could I possibly have known that a season of football with a bunch of high school kids— really a season of life more than anything else—would ultimately help me open doors to my own father that had always been sealed shut?

Chapter Two

THE WHOLE IMPROBABLE CHAIN OF EVENTS STARTED with a brief newspaper story that froze me at the breakfast table. The Maryland Board of Public Works had just approved a demolition contract—a wrecking ball would soon be bearing down on Memorial Stadium in Baltimore. I was lucky not to choke on my Cheerios. To me, that old stadium was so much more than just a tired collection of concrete and brick in an equally worn neighborhood. The people of Maryland were about to obliterate a shrine.

The little boy in me—unmindful of the grown-ups' rule that virtually nothing lasts forever—felt an immediate wave of sadness. Soon, though, the melancholy yielded to a rush of wonderful memories from my childhood days as a ball-boy with the Baltimore Colts. Wanting to put my hands on something tangible from those days long gone, I went upstairs to my bedroom and dug through a collection of old photos and other keepsakes cluttering the top drawer of my dresser. I found some snapshots I'd taken when I was eleven years old, very large men wearing football gear, frozen in black-and-white Kodak squares for more than a quarter of a century. I smiled when I came across a shot of Joe Ehrmann trudging off the practice field at training camp during the summer of 1974, big mop of brown hair all disheveled after being liberated from his helmet, Popeye-like forearms sticking out from the elbow-length sleeves of a dark number 76 jersey, which I knew to be royal blue,

Colts blue. I also found a few old football cards, some Colts bumper stickers, and an assortment of stadium passes that once gave me access to locker rooms and fields wherever the Colts were playing. There was something about going through those knickknacks that made me feel warm and whole.

I wanted to make a farewell visit to Memorial Stadium, just had to see and feel the place one last time, so I called an editor friend at the *Baltimore Sun* and asked about contributing a story from the perspective of a former ballboy. He was kind enough to indulge me with an assignment, and a state official agreed to open the doors for me.

It was a brisk Friday morning in January 2001, almost seventeen years after the Colts moved to Indianapolis, when I left my Washington, D.C., home for the one-hour drive to 33rd Street in Northeast Baltimore. Just after nine o'clock, I pulled into an empty parking lot and slowly circled my childhood home away from home. Windows were boarded up. Walls were filled with graffiti. The long-vacant building was hermetically sealed, but I was soon joined by Ed Cline, deputy director of the Maryland Stadium Authority, who had keys.

"Bring a flashlight?" he asked me.

"All set," I said.

We walked through the old Colts locker room. It was cold and empty, not a single visual clue as to who used to inhabit the space. Cline made sure that the tunnel from the locker room out to the field was safe for passage. Then I was on my own. The dark, narrow tunnel was even smaller than I remembered it. But this was not a walk to be measured in anything as finite as height or distance. It was to be measured only in the comfort of fond memories. The first time I made that walk was on Friday, August 9, 1974, when the

Colts played a pre-season game. It was the same day Richard Nixon resigned the presidency. How could I even guess the number of times I navigated that tunnel throughout the remainder of my childhood? I could still vividly imagine the loud click-clacking of cleats striking the concrete floor as my Colts marched in and out of battle. It was a defining sound of my youth.

At the end of the tunnel, I climbed the six steps to field level and entered . . . a ghost town. The grass field was long gone. I walked on pea-size gravel and black patches of ice, working my way around tall, brown weeds, some climbing higher than my waist, as I surveyed the scarred remnants of glory. Most of the stadium seats had been ripped out. The giant scoreboard had been stripped bare. The landscape was littered with garbage. I walked slowly around the horseshoe-shaped structure, especially savoring my steps along the old Colts sideline. I stood where one of my best friends on the team, Toni Linhart, kicked a field goal through the fog to beat the Miami Dolphins in an epic overtime game in 1975. I lingered where I used to play catch with the star quarterback, Bert Jones, the NFL's Most Valuable Player in 1976.

After half an hour of absolute solitude in a place that had routinely rocked with the high-octane energy of sixty thousand fans, I was back at the stairs to the tunnel. I took in a deep breath and tried to soak up my final vision of Memorial Stadium. More than anything else, though, I kept thinking about the players with whom I had worked and traveled and even shared a dormitory during summer training camps. So many had taken the time to care about me, to help me learn and grow. I had always kept in touch with a few former Colts. But now I wondered about the rest who had played during my ten years, 1974 through 1983, on the sidelines. What were they doing with their lives?

Walking out of Memorial Stadium for the last time—the rising sun barely peeking over the closed end of the upper deck—I knew exactly what I wanted to do. I wanted to find my Colts. Of course, I had no way of knowing what it would mean to be reunited with Joe Ehrmann.

Chapter Three

WE FIRST MET EARLY THAT SUMMER OF 1974. I HAD just finished sixth grade. Joe Ehrmann was preparing for his second season with the Colts.

I never planned on meeting Joe or anyone else on the team. When my parents drove me down to Baltimore from our hometown of Rye Brook, New York, a small suburb just north of New York City, I had only one thing in mind: having fun. I was going to a tennis camp at McDonogh School.

It was not until I arrived that I found out the Colts would conduct their pre-season training camp on the same grounds. The football practice fields were right next to the tennis courts. That allowed for my up-close-and-personal introduction to professional sports. At first I was just an anonymous kid asking for autographs and taking pictures. But then—just by hanging around before and after practices—I actually got to know most of the guys on the team. I was an outgoing, polite little kid who never really wanted anything beyond their attention and acceptance, and even though a good number of them seemed almost superhuman to me, they still made me feel comfortable in their world. Some of the players came to treat me like a little brother. They played catch with me. They took me to Baskin-Robbins for ice cream. They talked to me about all the important things in life, mainly sports and girls. After a while, the Colts equipment man and trainers were so used to having me around that they let me help with minor tasks such as hanging jerseys in lockers, handing out towels, and pouring Gatorade.

The ultimate highlight was the first time I went to Memorial Stadium with the Colts. For the team it was a meaningless pre-season loss to the Detroit Lions. For me it was the most amazing experience any sports-loving kid could ever imagine. After the game, I cut loose the yellow field pass tied to a belt loop on my shorts. That pass was going home with me—proof that I had not been dreaming.

I also took a poem and a nickname back to New York.

The poem came from a sign hanging outside the Colts locker room at McDonogh. I had no idea who first wrote the words or when they were written. I only knew that I had read them many times and never wanted to forget them. So I borrowed a pencil and notepad from one of the coaches and copied them in the shaky handwriting of childhood.

That Guy in the Glass

When you get what you want in your struggle for self
and the world makes you king for a day,
then go to the mirror and look at yourself
and see what that guy has to say.

For it isn't your mother, brother or friends
whose judgment you must pass.
the person whose verdict counts most in your life
is the one staring back in the glass.

You can go down the pathway of years
receiving pats on the back as you pass.
but your final reward will be heartaches and tears
if you cheated that guy in the glass.

When I was done writing, I carefully folded up my "Guy in the Glass" and tucked it in a pocket for safekeeping. I would eventually post it on a bulletin board in my bedroom, right next to a team picture of the 1974 Colts.

As for the nickname, it was definitely a strange one. The first time I heard it, I was sitting with some of the players on a hill by the practice fields.

"Hey, Brillo."

I ignored it at first, not realizing it was me that Joe Ehrmann was addressing.

But Joe could never be ignored for too long. On the field, he was relentless, the proud owner of a stubborn streak—opponents might say *mean* streak—that made him extremely tough to block. Off the field, though, the tough shell gave way to the fun-seeking free spirit within. Joe was not only one of the hardest workers on the team. He was also the life of the party, an enchanting blend of warmth and wittiness, and he was always reaching out to pull someone else in. He was one of those guys who coaches called "the glue" holding together the team.

"Hey, Jeff," Joe said, playfully pawing at the top of my Afro-adorned head with one of his impossibly thick hands. "Little white kid like you, where'd you get all that curly hair?"

"I don't know," I said.

"Ever thought about doing a commercial for those Brillo pads?"

Joe laughed, a deep, hearty laugh. We all laughed. And now I had a nickname. I was Brillo—not the most flattering moniker imaginable, but at least it was unique and therefore unforgettable. The Colts would always remember Brillo, and I could not possibly ask for anything more than that.

Once camp was over and I was home for the start of seventh grade, I did the best I could to keep in touch with my new football friends. I wrote a lot of letters, and sometimes when I bugged my parents enough, they allowed me to make a few long-distance phone calls. When the Colts came to play in New York, I helped in the locker room and on the sideline. Each of the next few years I helped at a game or two, and when I was sixteen, finally old enough for actual employment, the Colts hired me for the first of four summers as a full-time ballboy.

"Ballboy. A euphemism. The ballboy is the jack-of-all-dirty-jobs in a football training camp. Pick up towels, pick up jocks, launder socks, shine shoes, haul ice, sweep the floor, be there before the players, stay late. Long hours, hard work—heaven." That's how it was once described in a book about the Colts. And the conclusion was exactly right. I spent my summers in heaven.

Part of it was just the excitement of being on the inside of something so grand. But being with the Colts went far beyond the constant brush with greatness. It taught me invaluable lessons about the adult world. I learned that a man could at once be both intensely independent and an unselfish team player. I learned that skin color and other labels of division—geographic background, financial status, religious orientation—really meant nothing at all when it came to the contributions any individual might make. I learned that grown men could experience, and even exhibit, the full range of human emotions.

As the son of a stoic, that was a major revelation for me. My father, Richard Marx, was remarkably dedicated to all three of his children. He was supportive, kind, patient, gentle, steady . . . but much more rational than emotional. Highs and lows were for a weatherman reporting the temperature; my dad's emotional thermometer was generally stuck somewhere in the moderate middle. I always knew that he had strong beliefs because he showed them through his actions, never wavering in his commitments to family, to always doing the right thing, and especially to treating other people well. But actually talk about his feelings and emotions—express them in words? No. That was a foreign concept for my dad. Even his job—actuary for a life insurance company, a numbers cruncher—was a perfect extension of putting the rational before the emotional.

I never could have imagined my dad crying after being cut by a football team. I never could have pictured him celebrating with reckless abandon the outcome of a sporting event—or anything else for that matter. I never could have conjured up a set of circumstances that would have enabled my dad to speak freely with me about a girl I liked or to discuss the general concept of love. With the Colts, I saw and did all those things with men who sometimes felt like supplementary fathers. I learned that it was okay to *feel* and to express my feelings.

That would never be mistaken for the primary promotional message of the NFL. But it was a big part of my behind-the-scenes experience with professional football—and Joe Ehrmann played a major role in that.

"Brillo," Joe would bellow from high above my small frame. Joe always had a big smile and an equally high-wattage greeting for me. He might as well have been injecting me with some magical formula that offered instant acceptance and inclusion. Sometimes he would share a joke with me. Sometimes he would tease me the way an irrepressible brother goes after the little guy in the family, just for the

heck of it, nothing serious. In addition to the fun stuff, whenever I saw Joe during the regular season, meaning I was back in school in New York, he wanted to know how I was doing in my classes. "Doing great," I would tell him, and he always made me feel so good about that. In fact, he was an endless source of affirmation. In training camp, I might be doing something as menial as carting equipment out to the field, but Joe would somehow make me feel proud of my insignificant contributions. He would say, "Way to go, man, glad you're here, Brillo," and the echo of his words could spend hours bouncing around in my head.

After being picked in the first round of the 1973 NFL draft, Joe played for the Colts through 1980. He was co-captain of the team and became an All-Pro while leading a celebrated defensive line known as the Sack Pack. But it was really Joe's giant personality—not his ability to knock people down and mess up an offense—that made him such a wonderful character.

Joe was always pulling some sort of a prank. Teammates beware: Those inviting doughnuts on a table in the locker room might have been surreptitiously glazed in a tub of paraffin the trainers used for strictly non-dietary purposes such as treating a hand injury. Or perhaps Joe was loading up the bottom of a football with a fistful of mud while nobody was looking.

Away from the field, he was unofficial social director for the Colts. On Wednesday nights, Joe was the gregarious host of a poker game during which a firm grip on a cold beer or a tightly rolled reefer easily trumped the possession of, say, the king or queen of hearts. He was also the vibrant ringleader when it came to full-scale team parties. Then unmarried, Joe told people he had bought a big house "just with team parties in mind." Yes, the ridiculous-looking guy dressed as a toilet for the annual Halloween affair—that was Joe at his absolute best.

He was constantly working on material for his irreverent Bonehead of the Week Awards, which he presented to teammates in honor of their most embarrassing moments. A personal favorite: the spiked dog collar he ceremoniously wrapped around the neck of wide receiver Brian DeRoo during a team meeting just days after a coach had placed DeRoo in a temporary choke hold while cussing him out for a botched play.

Most of the players preferred the solitude and sameness of suburbia, but Joe shared his late nights with hippies and bikers in what he called the "freak scene" watering holes in a no-dress-code, no-rules section of town called Fells Point. Joe's nocturnal "uniform" was fairly standard: old pair of blue jeans; loose-fitting T-shirt, sometimes covered with a flannel button-down or sweatshirt; Colts-issued turf shoes with little rubber grippers on the soles; and his trademark brown-leather cap. It did not exactly come as a shock when a newspaper writer in Buffalo, New York, one of his hometown guys, placed Joe on an annual "Pro Football All-Everything List" as one of the worst-dressed players in the NFL. A friend was quoted as saying, "If Joe ever donates his clothes to the Salvation Army, they'll turn him down."

Joe's favorite Fells Point spots were Leadbetters Tavern and Turkey Joe's (no connection to his own name). He was equally comfortable squeezing into a booth with friends or dwarfing a bar stool alongside people he'd never met—just as long as the alcohol never ran dry and the conversation kept flowing. Sure, he was still Joe Ehrmann, number 76 of the home team, when he ventured down to Fells Point. He could never make himself anonymous in a city that revered its football team the way Baltimore cherished its Colts. But this was a part of town where he could also act and feel like the ordinary Joe he truly was. He was the son of a union man, a foreman on drill boats that traveled the Great Lakes and other waters, who was painfully absent during most of Joe's childhood. Joe was raised primarily by his mother and grandmother. He was a product of the city streets as much as he was a student of old P.S. 60 and Riverside High School in Buffalo. Joe even had a tattoo—a wolf peering out from high on his right arm, with his childhood nickname, Rookie, in bold letters below it, a fairly radical adornment in those days. All of this made him feel right at home with the colorful blue-collar folks at Leadbetters and Turkey Joe's.

"Free spirit?" Joe once wondered aloud during a rare interlude of introspection. "I don't know. I see myself as being free in the sense that I don't have a lot of responsibilities. I'm not tied to a lot of things . . . pretty carefree and casual. And I like to party. I like to party a lot."

But then all the partying came to a sudden stop.

Chapter Four

EIGHTEEN-YEAR-OLD BILLY EHRMANN FILLED TWO vital roles in Joe's life: brother and best friend. Ten years behind the star of the family, Billy had always worshipped his only brother. Whenever Billy had any sort of a problem, he would look to Joe for a solution, and Joe always seemed to have just the right answer. In turn, Joe felt the pride of a father as he watched Billy navigating the challenges of being a teenager. "No question," Joe would say. "It's gotta be the greatest thing in the world to have a brother."

And so the brothers Ehrmann were equally excited about the summer of 1978. Joe was at the top of his game—he was even being featured on the cover of the new Colts yearbook—and Billy was coming down from Buffalo to work in the team training camp. First they would spend the summer together. Then Billy would live with Joe while attending school and playing football at nearby Towson State University.

That was the plan, anyway. Then fate got in the way.

Billy had just finished a workout one day at the Colts training camp when he first noticed the ugly bruises—dark and menacing—all over his upper torso and arms. He went to Joe, of course, and Joe figured Billy had probably just overdone it a bit, maybe busted some capillaries. Joe asked the team trainer to take a look, just to play it safe, and the trainer wanted Billy to see a doctor. Next thing Joe knew, after the results of initial tests were in, he was scrambling for a dictionary to look up what it meant that he and Billy were being referred to an oncologist. Billy had a wicked form of cancer called aplastic anemia. His bone marrow was not producing enough blood cells.

Everyone in the family was tested to see if there was a match for a bone marrow transplant. There was not. Chemotherapy was the only option. And none of the doctors held out much hope. The next five months—with Billy tucked away in room 356 at Johns Hopkins Hospital— would prove to be as close to hell as anything the Ehrmanns had ever experienced. Billy battled the best he could. Joe spent many nights crumpled up on a cot so his little brother would never be alone while undergoing the worst of his treatments. But what could Joe possibly do to make that damn disease go away? What could *anyone* do?

Joe simply glowed on the rare occasions when Billy announced that he actually had an appetite—maybe he'd like a milkshake or even his favorite shrimp dish from a local restaurant. And there were other shining moments. Nobody would ever forget the look of excitement on Billy's face when Colts executive Ernie Accorsi showed up at the hospital with a film projector and a borrowed copy of the new hit movie *Animal House,* which Billy had so badly wanted to see. There was also the day that Jimmy Irsay, college-age son of Colts owner Robert Irsay, delivered a stereo for Billy's hospital room. Whenever Billy felt up to it, he and Joe cranked the Rolling Stones. *Some Girls* was their favorite album. "Miss You" became something of an anthem for them. Oh, how Billy smiled and laughed while playing air guitar and belting out tunes right along with the Stones. Sometimes he could even forget where he was for a few minutes.

But the complications worsened and the pain became constant. Billy was literally disappearing—losing ten or more pounds a week. He was not a complainer. But sometimes the anger and frustration got the best of him and he could not escape the thought: *Why can't Joe fix this? Any problem I've ever had, Joe has always been able to fix it.* More than once Billy found himself hanging on to Joe, hugging him, gripping him, and pushing his words through tears: "Don't let me die. Please, don't let me die."

Joe had never felt so utterly powerless, had never felt such anguish, such emptiness and confusion, but all he could do was hold Billy tightly and declare his hope for a better day.

"It has to get better," Joe said. "*Has* to."

But he also knew that to be virtually impossible.

No, Billy's childhood dreams would never come true. He would never get to follow his big brother into professional football. They would never get the chance to start a business together.

For Joe, it was becoming difficult to embrace any thought whatsoever of the future. Sometimes he would find himself looking into the past for solace. He could just close his eyes and see himself being home from school for lunch, and little Billy, two or three years old, sitting in his lap the whole time he ate. He could see himself walking Billy up the street to hang out with friends at Riverside Park. He could see himself teaching Billy how to use a fishing rod and reel—and the proud smile rushing across Billy's face when the fish finally started biting for him. No matter what Joe could see in his mind's eye, though, no matter how enduring and refreshing the images from days long gone, now there was really nothing left to do but sit and wait.

One day, passing time in the hospital by reading a book, Joe was all but mesmerized by a passage from an old poem by Edwin Markham.

There is a destiny that makes us brothers;
None goes his way alone:
All that we send into the lives of others
Comes back into our own.

Joe read that quote over and over—wrapping himself in those words as if he were sinking at sea and they could somehow be used as a life jacket—and he knew right then that he would always carry the comfort of that passage with him. He knew that he would always try to live by those words.

When the end was imminent, Joe took Billy out of the hospital so he could spend whatever time was left at home. But first the Ehrmanns made one last stop on their way to Joe's house. It was Thursday, December 14, 1978. The Colts were preparing for practice at Memorial Stadium. As part of his final journey, Billy wanted to be with them one more time. A few players came out to the parking lot because Billy was too weak to walk. He had to be lifted out of the car and carried into the locker room. But Billy smiled quite a bit that morning. He sat in a whirlpool, which temporarily swallowed some of his aches and pains, and then a trainer provided additional relief by massaging his legs. Mostly, though, Billy was happy just to see everyone, just to visit with friends. Two days later, surrounded by love and resting peacefully in the home of his big brother, Billy Ehrmann took his final breath.

Early in the afternoon of Tuesday, December 19, 1978, turning away from the grave into which the body of Billy Ehrmann had just been lowered at Elmlawn Cemetery in Buffalo, Joe felt a cool wind whipping across his face and found himself struggling with some of life's most difficult questions: If there truly is a God who loves us, how could he allow this to happen? How can there be so much suffering and so much unfairness in this world? What is the purpose of life? Where does real meaning—real value—come from?

Having been raised in a home with only a limited sampling of religious instruction, Joe had long before carved out for himself a framework of life in which the sport of football, its attendant fame and fortune included, offered the only salvation required. But now he needed something more. He needed answers to the most profound and complex questions he had ever encountered. Back in Baltimore, Joe started meeting with Larry Moody, unofficial team chaplain for the Colts, and the Bible became his constant companion. It carried Joe away from the party life and transformed him into a devout Christian. And this was only the beginning of his spiritual journey.

It was also soon after Billy's death that Joe and a local psychologist named Jay Levinson first met to discuss a project Levinson was hoping they could pursue together. Motivated by a story he had seen on television about the first Ronald McDonald House, in Philadelphia, Levinson, a death and bereavement specialist, wanted to build a similar facility to house cancer patients and their families in Baltimore. He figured that Joe might be willing to share his personal story and celebrity status to help garner public support, and after listening to Levinson explain his vision, Joe's immediate response was: "Man, where were you and your house when my parents were sleeping on windowsills in Billy's room at Hopkins?"

Long before Billy's illness, Joe had established himself as the Colts go-to guy when it came to helping charities.

Nobody on the team did more community work than he did. But working on the Ronald McDonald House—raising money, organizing and speaking at public events, schmoozing with politicians and business leaders—gave Joe a new appreciation of just how powerful the platform of sports could be when put to good use. It also made him feel like he was starting to make something out of that quote he had read in the hospital: *"All that we send into the lives of others comes back into our own."*

Another result of Joe's work and his fast-developing friendship with Levinson was an introduction to the writing of an Austrian psychiatrist named Viktor Frankl, most notably his book *Man's Search for Meaning.* A survivor of the Nazi concentration camps, Frankl developed a school of psychiatry called logotherapy, which teaches that there are only a few primary avenues on which one arrives at meaning in life. One is "by creating a work or by doing a deed." Another is by learning that "even the helpless victim of a hopeless situation, facing a fate he cannot change, may rise above himself, may grow beyond himself, and by so doing change himself. He may turn a personal tragedy into a triumph." *Wow,* Joe thought. *This is me he was writing about. There is hope.*

Yes, on April 28, 1980, when Joe joined Baltimore Mayor William Donald Schaefer at the corner of Arch and Lexington Streets to announce the site of a new Ronald McDonald House, there was both hope and meaning.

There was also hard evidence of the most important lesson I learned while growing up with a professional football team. Being around sports as much as I was, both working with the Colts and as a competitive young athlete myself, I was accustomed to coaches routinely barking out clichés to inspire their troops. There was always something about dealing with "adversity"—how any great athlete, any successful person at all, must always be able to "take something bad and make it into something good." Well, it was one thing to hear someone speaking vaguely about that. It was something else altogether to see someone actually doing it.

Joe took the ultimate negative—death—and made something positive out of it for both himself and others. By showing me instead of telling me, Joe said more than he ever could have communicated with mere words.

Chapter Five

WE KEPT IN TOUCH THROUGH MY JUNIOR YEAR OF COL-
lege. The last time I saw Joe—spring of 1983—he had left
the NFL and was playing for the Chicago Blitz in the new
United States Football League. I was a journalism student at
nearby Northwestern University, so I visited Joe at the
Blitz's practice facility. We talked about what he called the
ongoing "metamorphosis" in his life. Joe was studying to
be a minister. Though he still maintained his permanent
residence in Baltimore, he would soon be spending the off-
season at Dallas Theological Seminary.

"No more hanging out at Fells Point, huh?" I said.

"No, no, none of that anymore," Joe said. "Whole new
deal now. I've just mellowed out. Went through the whole
nine yards of learning, I guess. But I think I've eventually
developed into exactly who I was really supposed to be."

Pretty amazing, I thought. *Talk about a guy who has
changed. Still just as warm and friendly and open as ever. But
also so serious now.*

Before I left that day, Joe and I talked about keeping in
touch.

"Let me know how you're doing in school," Joe said.
"Call anytime, Brillo."

I was sure that I would. In fact, I was certain that Joe
would always somehow remain in my life. But after that
one afternoon together, Joe and I lost contact. It was nothing either one of us ever made a conscious decision about.

It was just life—simply a case of two people taking divergent paths that might never again intersect. I was a college
kid hanging out at fraternity parties and just starting to
wonder where and how I might land my first job in the real
world. Joe was a husband and father who had already been
a professional athlete for a decade and was now well on his
way to a whole new existence as a minister. Once we were
done swapping updates about ourselves and our friends
from the Colts, where was the common ground? Where
could any further conversation possibly take us?

After graduation in 1984, I moved to Kentucky and went to
work as a newspaper reporter for the *Lexington Herald-
Leader*. I did a fair number of sports stories. But I also covered everything from murder and the courts to coal mining
and local politics. Editors were always looking for "a warm
body" to send out on a breaking story, and by practically
living in the newsroom, even a newcomer like me was able
to draw plenty of good assignments. I was soon moved up
to special projects—newsroom jargon for investigative
reporting—and then I was offered the coveted job of
Washington correspondent. In the fall of 1987, I moved to
Capitol Hill, where I wrote primarily about the people and
issues of Congress.

As part of my daily routine, I skimmed several newspa-
pers. What a pleasant surprise I found in *The New York Times*
on Sunday, January 8, 1989: a generous story under the
headline "Ex-Football Player Finds New Goal With an
Urban Ministry in Baltimore." It was all about "the
Reverend" Joe Ehrmann and his new inner-city community
center known as The Door (so named because Joe saw it as
"a means of entrance for people locked out of mainstream

society"). The headline and pictures alone gave me a jolt of joy. Almost six years after Joe and I had last been together, here was the gift of knowledge that he had never stopped following his dreams, and that he was already transforming them into something special.

The story began with this: "The Door officially opened just before Christmas, and about 175 adults and children from an East Baltimore neighborhood were warmly greeted by the bearded, 260-pound figure of the Reverend Joe Ehrmann. Mr. Ehrmann, a former defensive tackle for the Baltimore Colts, is taking on a foe far more menacing than an opposing lineman: the multi-faceted ills of the inner city. But he has a game plan."

The immediate agenda included tutoring sessions and computer training as well as drug education and a variety of recreational sports. There was also a food bank and a clothing program. There would later be parenting classes and group sessions on subjects such as race relations and economic empowerment. The whole idea was to create a non-denominational, non-threatening setting in which entire families could be served, a comfortable, safe place where young and old alike could always find a sense of hope.

"In planning The Door and searching for suitable quarters, Mr. Ehrmann regularly attended Sunday services at the area's many storefront churches," the *Times* story said. "He was a stranger at first and frequently the only white person present in the congregations of a neighborhood that is predominantly black. Identifying himself at these services as an ordained minister, he invariably was asked to speak. He used the opportunities to talk about The Door. Now he is no longer a stranger."

It would have been one thing to operate The Door as a drop-by do-gooder sprinkling the neighborhood with char-

ity by day and then bathing himself in luxury—elsewhere—
at night. But that never would have worked for Joe, never
would have felt right. So he and his wife, Paula, then parents of two children, five-year-old Esther and one-year-old
Barney, moved from suburban Cockeysville into a row
house two blocks from The Door. Joe saw the new environment as a boon for little Esther and Barney.

"They get to have friends who are affluent and friends
who are poverty-stricken," he said. "They get to walk
through both worlds, and I hope they'll pick out the best of
both and do away with prejudice and stereotypes. They're
getting to see mankind as it's supposed to be."

Many more newspaper and magazine stories were later
written about Joe, usually focused on The Door, but sometimes they told of his work with some other civic or church
group. That was how I followed Joe through the years—by
seeing him pop up in print. Once in a while, I'd also hear
something about him from one of the former Colts with
whom I stayed in touch. But that was it. Even though Joe
was only an hour up the highway from Capitol Hill, and I
was often in Baltimore visiting friends, it never crossed my
mind to pick up the phone and call him. He was doing his
thing. I was doing mine.

It was only after my farewell visit to Memorial Stadium
that I finally had an incentive to contact the Reverend Joe
Ehrmann.

Chapter Six

MY PERSONAL THIRST FOR NOSTALGIA CERTAINLY COULD have been quenched by selecting perhaps a dozen favorite players and swapping memories by telephone. But that never would have satisfied the journalist in me. To give Baltimore football fans the type of story I now wanted to write for the *Sun*, I would have to speak with as many Colts as I could possibly find. I wanted to gather material for vignettes on their favorite Memorial Stadium memories and also a complete listing of "where they are now" updates.

Working from a collection of Colts media guides I excavated from deep in a closet, I made an alphabetical list of every player in uniform for at least one game during the ten years I was involved. From offensive lineman Sid Abramowitz to linebacker Steve Zabel, the list stretched to 212 names. The search was on.

Two weeks into the project I came to call "Dialing for Colts," I set my sights on Joe Ehrmann. A woman at The Door told me that Joe had not worked there for years, but she suggested that I try a place called Grace Fellowship Church. I was quite pleased when a church receptionist said that Joe was indeed a pastor there. I left him a voice mail: "Joe, this is Jeff Marx, as in Brillo." It was a nickname I had long since excised—and clearly a misnomer now that I'd been bald for years—but I wanted to make sure that Joe would know who was calling. Jeff Marx, he might not remember from a time and place so distant. Brillo, he would never forget.

Joe soon became the eighty-fifth former Colt with whom I spoke for my story. All I needed was an update on what he was doing and a favorite memory from Memorial Stadium. Then I would ask Joe if he had any information to help me find more Colts. Simple as that. But our conversation was by no means routine. We talked for almost an hour.

Most of the other guys I had reached could be neatly packaged in a box: business owner, salesman, teacher, firefighter, factory worker, whatever. Although Joe was usually identified as an ordained minister before anything else, his activities were much too eclectic for any assumptions or restrictions that come with a single label. Joe was "a preaching pastor in church," as he put it. But he was also a high school football coach. And he was running a foundation called Building Men for Others, which he had created with a friend. Joe was the most animated when telling me about the foundation.

With The Door, he had tried to tackle all the worst ills of society at once. Poverty, racism, drugs, crime, illiteracy, family disintegration—Joe saw and heard all the horror stories imaginable and kept helping as many folks as he could. He and The Door were widely recognized with numerous awards and prominent visitors including George W. Bush. But Joe finally reached a conclusion that pushed him in a new direction: *All these problems I've been trying to deal with, they're not just problems, they're also symptoms,* he came to realize. *They're symptoms of the single biggest failure of our society. We simply don't do a good enough job of teaching boys how to be men.*

"If we do not help boys become men, then we really won't be able to fix anything else in this country," Joe told me on the phone. With Building Men for Others, Joe was teaching boys his own definition of masculinity and a code of conduct for manhood. I was intrigued. I scribbled notes as Joe spoke. But I also mentally drifted as I pondered the depth of what he was telling me. Others had been filling my notebook with favorite memories, football nuggets; Joe was sharing poignant chunks of life.

Toward the end of our conversation, Joe patiently fielded my queries about former Colts for whom I was still looking. Two of them were members of his church. Beyond that, Joe had only sketchy leads on a few guys, which surprised me. I would have guessed that he had stayed connected with more of his teammates. Joe had an explanation, though, and it was one that surprised me. Despite any outward appearances to the contrary, regardless of all the rah-rah team bonding and locker room camaraderie associated with professional football, it is a setting that does not often foster substantive, enduring friendships.

"It's pseudo-community, it's the pretense of being in community, but it's really not being in community," Joe said. "It's all environmentally driven. So we'd play cards together. We'd party together. We'd chase girls together. We'd talk about making money together and doing 'power' things together. But very few sustainable relationships ever come out of all that."

Joe asked me a question that initially seemed to be strangely out of place in our conversation: Had I read Richard Ben Cramer's recently published biography of baseball great Joe DiMaggio? I had not. But I had heard about it. I knew that it painted a pathetic picture of a much-celebrated public hero—the legendary Yankee Clipper, dapper husband of Marilyn Monroe—who was anything but heroic in his private life.

"Well, more than anything, it's the story of a man's search for a heart," Joe said. "And that's really a journey that an awful lot of athletes go through, an awful lot of men, period, because we're searching based on all the wrong things—money, fame, power."

Joe had the DiMaggio book on his mind because he had just attended a lunch with its author. But now I began to understand the thought process that prompted Joe to bring it up with me. He had started with a simple observation, my surprise that he was not still in touch with more of his old teammates, and he had sent it through a prism that had come to filter just about everything in his life. The prism was his profound understanding of what it really means, really *ought* to mean, to be a man. First and foremost is the ability to enter and maintain meaningful relationships. It was that understanding that catapulted Joe from my casual observation into his sociological critique of professional football. And it was that understanding that provided the context for offering his thoughts on the DiMaggio book.

Clearly, we had moved well beyond the scope of anything I would ever use in a newspaper story about Memorial Stadium and the Colts. But I wanted to know more about Joe. I wanted to know more about Building Men for Others.

This time there was no way I would let eighteen years slip by between phone calls.

Chapter Seven

JOE EHRMANN IN A TUXEDO? THIS WAS THE SAME GUY who used to confront the team dress code for road trips by sporting one of those silly T-shirts with a tie printed down the front. Now he was the very definition of conformity. His laborious gait was also new to me. So was that white hair . . . and those glasses. But those welcoming brown eyes were the same as always. It felt good to see Joe's face lighting up as he greeted me.

"Hey, Jeff."

"Great to finally see you," I said.

"Great to see *you*, man. Been a while, huh?"

We chatted briefly. Then someone tugged at Joe. He was needed across the room.

This was a Tuesday evening in March 2001. A few weeks after I had first reached Joe at his church, we both happened to be at a big fund-raising dinner in a Baltimore banquet hall. We were there for the twenty-third annual Ed Block Courage Awards, named after the late Colts trainer and dedicated to supporting programs for abused children. The award, among the most prestigious in professional football, is presented to one player from each NFL team. I was at the banquet because I was still searching for Colts and some of them were expected. Joe was there because he had long been intimately involved with the Ed Block Awards. In 1978, he was the first recipient. Standing at the podium that night, Joe shared the honor with brother Billy by making a telephone call to his hospital room, and their conversation was piped through the sound system for all to hear. All these years later, Joe now served as chaplain for the Ed Block program.

After cocktails and mingling, the 2001 honorees were individually introduced into a mammoth room filled with seventeen hundred diners. Then Joe approached the long dais and settled at center stage.

"Well, good evening," he said. "Why don't you turn to somebody next to you and say, 'We're here because of children.'" Some did as asked, reciting his words, but most just sat and stared. "Let's go ahead and pray," Joe said, bowing his head. "Almighty God, good Father, we thank you that we come here this evening as one family, in the spirit of Ed Block, who taught us how to live and to love. We thank you that every child in this world is created in your image, filled with dignity and status and potential. Unite our hearts, unite our minds, unite our souls, that where children are neglected or abandoned or abused, that we as a human community would step up to help them reach their fullest potential and to participate in this world. Bless this evening. And we give you thanks. Amen."

My thoughts drifted back to game days with the Colts. The team always huddled together in the locker room—both before and after playing—and recited the Lord's Prayer: *"For thine is the kingdom, and the power, and the glory, for ever and ever."* I felt the warmth and comfort of a cocoon when I was down on a knee with the Colts. I thought of that now because after Billy died, Joe was always the one who led the team in prayer. Hearing him speak in that banquet hall, I felt for an instant that his words had carried me back to my childhood.

———

Knowing that I wanted to find out more about Building Men for Others, Joe soon invited me to meet him one afternoon in College Park, Maryland, where he was speaking at a University of Maryland football clinic. Joe was on the stage in a campus auditorium, preparing to address about two hundred high school coaches, when one of them approached with a question.

"You gonna be talking about offense, or defense?"

Joe's answer surprised this man who'd been expecting a chalk talk focused on the X's and O's of football diagrams.

"Philosophy," Joe said. "I'll be talking about how to help boys become men within the context of sports."

After introductory remarks, Joe started into the substance of his speech: "I spent thirteen years in professional football. And when I look back over my career, I have to say that the thing that impacted me the most, that I've taken away out of the game into my current life, really, is this concept of team. In the NFL, what you have is fifty-three men— black men and white men, men from the inner cities, from the suburbs, from the farmlands of America—and they're able to come together every year and kind of set aside their own personal goals, wants and ambitions, in order to put the team first. And I think that's the challenge, really, facing us in this society, is how we learn to come together, across all racial, economic, and geographical divisions, to make this society a much better place.

"I have spent almost the last twenty years as a minister. Most of my work is in the inner city of Baltimore, dealing with issues of poverty and systemic racism and family disintegration. At the end of all these years, I would say that in order to make America a more just and fair society, I would boil it down to the single greatest crisis. If we don't address this issue, we really can't deal with the other issues. And that primary, critical issue is a concept of what it means to be a man. If we don't fix our understanding, and get some proper definition of masculinity and manhood, I don't think we can address other issues.

"So I am part of a football program in Baltimore, and we use this as our base philosophy. Our understanding is that sports—football—is nothing more than a context to help connect with boys and teach them, one, a clear and compelling definition of what it means to be a man. Second is to give them a code of conduct for manhood. And then third is to help them figure out what their own unique, transcendent cause should or could be in this world."

If all of this was still a bit vague to an unexpectant audience that was hearing Joe for the first time, he promised to elaborate on the broad points he had just introduced. First, though, Joe wanted to share more of his personal background.

"My mother raised four children," Joe said. "I did not really know my father till I was well into my high school years. I have a few memories of him, but all of them are extremely painful. I was a kid that grew up in a difficult situation, with many needs, both in the house and out in our community. And I always saw football as kind of a way out for me."

Joe talked about the remarkable path that football did indeed pave for him—from Buffalo to "Big Man on Campus" at Syracuse University, from there to a hefty contract and star status in the NFL. Unfortunately, Joe said, the entire journey was littered with "tremendous chaos and turmoil" because he never really felt that he belonged in "the different strata and spheres" associated with economic success and fame.

"I had expectations that professional football would

help me find some kind of purpose and meaning in my life," he said. "But, really, all I found in the NFL was more confusion. I kept having the belief that if it wasn't going to be this contract, I would certainly find some kind of serenity or peace in my life with the next contract, the next girl, the next house, the next car, the next award, *when* I got to the Pro Bowl, *when* we got to the Super Bowl. And what happened to me, I think it happens to an awful lot of professional athletes: You start losing perspective. You've kind of climbed the ladder of success, and when you get up there, you realize somehow the ladder was leaning on the wrong building."

This was the first time I'd ever heard Joe talk about anything like this. As a kid, I never would have known that Joe had such troubling issues bubbling below the surface. But I could see exactly where he was now taking his audience. Joe was setting up the big turning point in his life. Billy's story was next. Joe told it with passion.

"I was absolutely devastated," he said. "I was devastated by the reality of losing the person that I loved the most in this entire world. And I was equally devastated by the reality that all the things that I had invested my life in really couldn't help him one bit."

Joe explained how losing his brother started him down a new path. Buoyed by his theological training and inner-city ministerial work, it was a journey that ultimately led to the philosophy behind Building Men for Others and his work as a coach at Gilman School. As Joe told his audience, it is a philosophy that applies to all boys, no matter what type of parents they have or where they start in terms of socioeconomic factors.

"I think that the boys you are coaching—all boys—are given in our culture a threefold criteria for what it means to be a man," he said. "I think those are a lie, and I think they lead to tremendous dysfunction both in marriages and relationships, and in the social problems of America."

Joe discussed the three components of what he termed "false masculinity": athletic ability, sexual conquest, and economic success. After debunking the supposed value of that triumvirate, he introduced his own paradigm for masculinity.

"Masculinity, first and foremost, ought to be defined in terms of relationships," Joe said. "It ought to be taught in terms of the capacity to *love* and to *be* loved. If you look over your life at the end of it . . . life wouldn't be measured in terms of success based on what you've acquired or achieved or what you own. The only thing that's really going to matter is the relationships that you had. It's gonna come down to this: What kind of father were you? What kind of husband were you? What kind of coach or teammate were you? What kind of son were you? What kind of brother were you? What kind of friend were you? Success comes in terms of relationships.

"And I think the second criterion—the only other criterion for masculinity—is that all of us ought to have some kind of cause, some kind of purpose in our lives that's bigger than our own individual hopes, dreams, wants, and desires. At the end of our life, we ought to be able to look back over it from our deathbed and know that somehow the world was a better place because we lived, we loved, we were other-centered, other-focused."

Joe spoke about several elements of his code of conduct for manhood: accepting responsibility, leading courageously, enacting justice on behalf of others. He touched on the importance of instilling in boys the concept of empathy. Then he discussed what he called the "leukemia of masculinity"—the combination of nurturing wounds and shame—that often keeps boys and men blocked off from their true potential.

"There's an awful lot of nurturing wounds," Joe said. "In my experience, I would say that the number-one common denominator of professional football players—and I think this is true throughout most sports, I think it's true in the boardrooms of America—that the number-one common denominator is this father-and-son dysfunction. I think we have an awful lot of sons that are trying to validate and earn the love and respect from their fathers through some kind of performance, be it athletic or otherwise."

Joe defined shame in general terms: "Shame is a concept not that you do wrong things. See, when you do wrong things, you can always make amends or give apologies. Concepts of shame are not that I do bad things, but that somehow when God made me, my initial make-up was all wrong."

To illustrate his point, Joe unleashed one of the most personal, painful stories I'd ever heard in such a public setting: his earliest memory of his father.

"I was about the age of five or six," Joe said. "My father was an ex-professional boxer and then was kind of a traveling stevedore on the Great Lakes. And he would come back into the house every few years. And I think what he felt was that it was his responsibility to come in and to make sure that I was growing up as a man. My father's concept of masculinity was that men don't cry, men don't feel, men don't need, men don't touch—that if you really want to be a man, you learn how to dominate and control.

"So the earliest memory I have of my father was him taking me down into the basement. He'd put up his hands." Joe held up his own now, palms open toward the audience, like a traffic cop making twin stop signals. "I'd have to stand there, and I'd have to learn how to throw these jabs and combinations. And I can remember trying to hit those just right. And then my father would start slapping me. He'd start slapping me to the point where tears were just coming down my face. And then what my father did to me was he *shamed* my sense of masculinity. Because what he told me was that men don't cry! Suck it up!" Joe was no longer speaking his words so much as he was spitting them out, voice raised, cadence intensified. "Be tough! Don't be a girl! Don't be a sissy! You gotta learn how to give a punch and *take* a punch in this world!"

Joe paused. The room was dead silent for a few moments until he continued, once again calm and deliberate: "I think I stood there as a young boy, when I knew my father was coming home, I think all I wanted my father to do was to walk into my life, embrace me, look me in the eye, and tell me that he loved me. But when he gave me this message—that I wasn't quite man enough because of the emotions and the tears—I had this concept that whatever the stuff was that makes up men, somehow God had put all this feminine emotion in me. And I think for young boys, if they feel they don't have the right *stuff*, they learn to live with the right *bluff*."

That last word seemed to bounce forever off the walls in this cavernous room. The only other scattered noises were the sounds of a few men squirming in their seats. Perhaps they were flashing back to certain childhood memories of their own. Joe would later tell me that whenever he starts opening up about his father during a speech or a workshop or a sermon, that is when he always sees the eyes start welling up and it feels like all the air is being sucked out of the room. That is when he knows for sure that he is hitting on something much bigger and broader than the singular pain of his own personal reflections.

"I would say that if you ever wanted to create a professional athlete, it's those basement kinds of experiences," Joe said. "Because that would dictate the rest of my adolescent and early adult life. When I went out for high school football, it wasn't about camaraderie. It wasn't about having fun. It wasn't being part of the school or the community. For me, it was a life-and-death issue of trying to validate my masculinity. I felt that I validated myself as a man every time I knocked you flat on your back. But I tell you, those kinds of concepts, they don't make good husbands, they don't make good fathers, they don't make good sons, and they don't make good friends. They leave boys in a tremendous sense of confusion."

Joe said that the Gilman football staff had an absolute rule about shaming. There will be none. It is the first item on a fourteen-point code of conduct Joe put in writing for himself and his colleagues: "Let us be mindful to never shame a boy, but to correct him in an uplifting and loving way. Affirmation!"

Someone in the audience asked a question that was probably on the minds of more than a few men in the room: All this stuff sounds great, but what about winning and losing? Kids still play high school football because they want to win, right?

"Well, we've had great success the last few years," Joe said, without mentioning the specifics of back-to-back undefeated seasons (1998 and 1999) that had catapulted Gilman to the top spot in the state rankings. "But we try to evaluate our staff two ways. One is our wins and losses. And the other is the amount of ministry that we've done with our kids."

Two things happened on my drive home that day.

I reacted to Joe's speech with some serious self-evaluation—mulling over my relationships with friends and family, taking mental inventory of the priorities in my life. And I wondered what it would be like to spend one more football season with Joe. As a child, I had learned so much from him. What might I learn from him now?

Chapter Eight

THE 2001 GILMAN FOOTBALL TEAM CAME TOGETHER for its first practice at eight in the morning on a warm and overcast Monday. It was August 13. After driving from Capitol Hill to the leafy Roland Park neighborhood of Baltimore—a forty-eight-mile trip I would repeat many times during the next three months—I was greeted by the familiar sound of cleats on concrete. It was the same sound that used to fill that tunnel at Memorial Stadium, only now it was the click-clacking of boys pounding a paved path en route to a secluded practice field tucked away in the woods behind their school. For the boys, the short walk through the woods opened up to a rectangular plot of land—striped with fresh white sidelines and yard markings—on which they would transform themselves from classmates into teammates, from friends into family. For me, the walk yielded an introduction to an unmistakably unique high school sports program—and to a season that captured both my mind and my heart in ways that I never could have anticipated.

When I arrived, Joe was standing in the near corner of the field, welcoming everyone back from summer vacation, sharing hugs and handshakes as if he were running for mayor.

"Hey, Coach Ehrmann."

"Great to see you, Coach Ehrmann."

It was strange to hear the boys addressing him that way.

I was still working on the transition from thinking of Joe as an "ex-Colt" to viewing him as a minister, "the Reverend Joe." Now he was "Coach Ehrmann" as well. Joe was the defensive coordinator. He was encircled by a few of the boys, introducing me around, when the shrill sound of a whistle violated the serenity of morning.

"Bring it up, boys." The booming voice prompted immediate scurrying toward the center of the nearby end zone. "Let's go. Everyone up."

The shouted instruction emanated from an oversized teddy bear of a man, big, thick guy with a buzz cut of brown hair, wearing baggy, nylon mesh shorts and a Gilman T-shirt with the sleeves cut away to free his massive upper arms. He was the head coach, Francis "Biff" Poggi, a former Gilman football player (class of 1979) and now a wealthy business owner who devoted much of his time to philanthropy. Financial management was his business—his local investment company, Samuel James Limited, had been quite successful in a wide range of public and private equity deals—but working with children was his passion. Biff was Joe's best friend and the man with whom he had started Building Men for Others. Their roles varied depending on the setting and context in which they were implementing their program for boys and men, but at Gilman they generally stuck with a single formula. Joe was the ecclesiastic authority who often stood in the shadows but always provided wisdom and guidance. Biff was the program's public face and its animated voice. And now it was time for his opening remarks to the team.

In a sense, the same scene was unfolding that very day, or perhaps it would happen in the next week or so, on high school fields throughout the nation. Tough guys of all shapes and sizes were strapping on helmets with the boundless excitement of youth and the anticipation that comes with the clean slate of a new year. On another level, though, what happened that first day at Gilman was entirely unlike anything normally associated with high school football. It started with the signature exchange of the Gilman football program—this time between Biff and the gathered throng of eighty boys, freshmen through seniors, who would spend the next week practicing together before being split into varsity and junior varsity teams.

"What is our job?" Biff asked on behalf of himself, Joe, and the eight other assistant coaches.

"To love us," most of the boys yelled back. The older boys had already been through this routine more than enough times to know the proper answer. The younger boys, new to Gilman football, would soon catch on.

"And what is *your* job?" Biff shot back.

"To love each other," the boys responded.

I would quickly come to realize that this standard exchange—always initiated by Biff or Joe—was just as much a part of Gilman football as running or tackling.

"I don't care if you're big or small, huge muscles or no muscles, never even played football or star of the team—I don't care about any of that stuff," Biff went on to tell the boys, who sat in the grass while he spoke. "If you're here, then you're one of us, and we love you. Simple as that."

Biff paused.

"Look at me, boys," he started again. Most of them were already staring up in at least the general direction of his six-foot-three, 300-pound frame. Thanks to the combination of his physical stature and his never-ending passion for both football and the overall well-being of his players—"my boys," he always called them—Biff never had much of a problem holding their attention. But he often used that "look at me" phrase as a rhetorical device to signal when something really important was coming.

"Look at me, boys," Biff said. "We're gonna go through this whole thing as a team. We are the Gilman football community. A *community*. This is the only place probably in your whole life where you're gonna be together and work together with a group as diverse as this—racially, socially, economically, you name it. It's a beautiful thing to be together like this. You'll never find anything else like it in the world—simply won't happen. So enjoy it. Make the most of this. It's yours."

Biff asked the boys to take a few moments and look around at one another. With heads swiveling, what they saw was indeed a melting pot of black and white, rich and poor, city and suburb. Though an elite private school for boys only, Gilman had long prided itself on diversity, and thanks to the effect of recruiting and a powerful equalizer known as financial aid, the football team offered an even better cross section of society than the overall student population.

Heads were still turning when Biff broke the silence with slowly spoken words strung together into chunks for emphasis: "The relationships you make here . . . you will always have them . . . for the rest of your life . . . the rest of your life."

Biff was speaking just above a whisper now. There was something magical about the spell of such a big, powerful man turning down the volume like that. His players were totally locked in.

"Cherish this, boys," Biff said. "Cherish this."

So what if The Associated Press had recently anointed Gilman as the top-ranked team in Maryland and *USA Today* had picked the Greyhounds for the pre-season Top Ten of the entire East? Gilman football did not exist for anyone on the outside looking in. It was not about public accolades. It was about living in community. It was about fostering relationships. It was about learning the importance of serving others. Oh, sure, Biff allowed that he was definitely in favor of beating archrival McDonogh—the same McDonogh at which I had spent that fateful summer of 1974 with the Colts. In fact, winning that one game and successfully defending the league championship (Conference A of the Maryland Interscholastic Athletic Association) were the only performance-related goals he announced to the boys. But such accomplishments would only be by-products of a much broader agenda. The only thing that really mattered to Biff and Joe was offering a solid foundation on which the boys could later construct lives of meaning and value.

I watched a variety of football drills and conditioning exercises during that first day on the field in the woods. I also listened in on offensive and defensive strategy sessions in the team meeting room on the second floor of the school's field house. At one point, I even heard the Reverend Joe Ehrmann temporarily abandon the soft language of his day job when he introduced the three P's expected of anyone who wanted to play defense for him. Penetrate. Pursue. Punish. "All eleven men flying to the ball," Joe said. "All eleven men. Every single play."

Still, no matter how much football I saw and heard during those initial hours of the season, I drove away thinking only about the philosophical overview Biff had shared with the boys during those first few minutes of the morning. If a Martian had just happened to land on Earth and somehow found himself witnessing only that introductory talk, a perfectly logical communique home might have included a summary such as this: "Learned about some sort of group gathering called football. It teaches boys to love."

Joe, Biff, and the boys had nineteen days to prepare for the first of ten games on their schedule. The toughest part of that stretch included both morning and afternoon practice sessions—"two-a-days" in football parlance—wrapped in the stifling heat and humidity of late summer. Standing on the sidelines and wandering around the field for a good number of those practices, there were times I felt like a kid again. Occasionally, during a break in the action, I would get one of the boys or one of the coaches to play catch for a few minutes. With the pebbled leather of a football both scuffing my palms and stoking my imagination, I might as well have been back in training camp with the Colts.

Of course, it never took too long to be reminded that my reality was now housed on a totally unfamiliar end of the age spectrum. With the Colts, I was a wide-eyed kid running around in an adult world filled with real-life action heroes. At Gilman, I was a grown man surrounded by football players still dealing with pimples and prom dates.

I initially found it disconcerting whenever one of the boys addressed me with a deferential "sir" or called me Mr. Marx. But spending time with them quickly proved to be an extremely refreshing experience. Without any children of my own, I enjoyed the burst of exposure to the rhythms and rituals of the teen years. The boys were so excitable. They were often hilarious. And they were always open to new thoughts and ideas—so inquisitive and ready to learn.

They could not have found two better men to serve as teachers.

Joe and Biff originally met in the mid-1970s, when Joe was with the Colts and Biff was a high school football player who sometimes found a way to sneak into the team training facility and lift weights with the pros. Though their only conversation was brief, Biff would always remember being charmed by the magnificent leader of the Sack Pack, and that alone made him feel personally connected whenever he saw Joe play at Memorial Stadium or on television. More than a decade later, after Joe had retired from football and Biff had completed his own playing days as an offensive lineman at Duke, the memory of that one chance encounter in the Colts' weight room remained fond enough for Biff to respond with great joy when he happened to see Joe back on television. It was around Thanksgiving. Biff was visiting his parents when Joe was interviewed for a feature story about The Door.

"Hey, Dad, we need to go down there," Biff said. "Can't we do something to help?"

They drove downtown to The Door, unannounced, with a sizable donation of food. Biff was pleased to find Joe there, and they struck up a conversation that has never really ended. The first project they did together was a football camp—part football, part education, actually—for kids from The Door. Then they started working together on a summer camp for disadvantaged youngsters in South Carolina, where Biff had a home. Over time, their wives became friends and their young sons started playing together. Joe and Biff became inseparable.

"We've always had an incredible bond," Biff told me. "It just seems like there's a bridge between our souls."

When I asked Joe about that, he said, "Biff is God's replacement for Billy."

Even the age difference—Joe now fifty-two, Biff forty-one—was about right.

Joe simply loved having a little brother again.

My favorite part of two-a-days was Biff's daily talks about Building Men for Others.

Prior to afternoon practices, the boys streamed into the meticulously maintained field house officially known as the Redmond C. S. Finney Athletic Center (named after a longtime Gilman headmaster) and climbed the stairs to the team meeting room, where they plopped themselves in chairs behind four long rows of tables. Large windows at the front of the room overlooked a cavernous gymnasium, but the blinds were generally kept closed. All eyes were on Biff. He usually began in a chair, facing the team from behind a small table of his own, but he often got up to use the grease-marker board waiting in a corner for him, and once standing, Biff typically paced for a while as he spoke. The talks usually lasted twenty to thirty minutes. I was the only one taking notes. Everyone else just listened.

There were times when Joe contributed a relevant story from the Bible to underscore a particular message Biff was sharing with the boys—and Biff sometimes injected a brief passage on his own. But the overriding themes were, if not entirely secular, certainly universal.

"I expect greatness out of you," Biff once told the boys. "And the way we measure greatness is the impact you make on other people's lives."

How would the boys make the most impact? Almost anything Biff ever talked about could be fashioned into at least a partial answer to that question.

For one thing, they would make an impact by being inclusive rather than exclusive.

"The rest of the world will always try to separate you," Biff said. "That's almost a law of nature—gonna happen no matter what, right? The rest of the world will want to sepa-

rate you by race, by socioeconomic status, by education lev-
els, by religion, by neighborhood, by what kind of car you
drive, by the clothes you wear, by athletic ability. You name
it—always gonna be people who want to separate by that
stuff. Well, if you let that happen now, then you'll let it happen later. Don't let it happen. If you're one of us, then you
won't walk around putting people in boxes. Not now. Not
ever. Because every single one of them has something to
offer. Every single one of them is special. Look at me, boys."

They were looking.

"We are a program of inclusion," Biff said. "We do *not*
believe in separation."

The boys would also make an impact by breaking down
cliques and stereotypes, by developing empathy and kindness for all.

"What's empathy?" Biff asked them. "Feeling what?"

"Feeling what the other person feels," said senior
Napoleon Sykes, one of the team captains, a small but solid
wide receiver and hard-hitting defensive back who had
already accepted a scholarship to play college football at
Wake Forest.

"Exactly right," Biff said. "Not feeling *for* someone, but
with someone. If you can put yourself in another man's
shoes, that's a great gift to have for a lifetime."

That was the whole idea behind Biff and Joe's ironclad
rule that no Gilman football player should ever let another
Gilman boy—teammate or not—eat lunch by himself.

"You happen to see another boy off by himself, go sit
with him or bring him over to sit with you and your
friends," Biff said. "I don't care if you know him or not. I
don't care if he's the best athlete in the school or the
so-called nerd with his head always down in the books. You
go get him and you make him feel wanted, you make him

feel special. Simple, right? Well, that's being a man built for others."

How else would the boys make an impact?

By living with integrity . . . and not only when it is con- venient to do so. Always.

By seeking justice . . . because it is often hidden.

By encouraging the oppressed . . . because they are always *dis*couraged.

Ultimately, Biff said, the boys would make the greatest overall impact on the world—would bring the most love and grace and healing to people—by constantly basing their thoughts and actions on one simple question: What can I do for *you*?

"Not, what can I do to get a bigger bank account or a bigger house?" Biff said. "Not, what can I do to get the pret- tiest girl? Not, what can I do to get the most power or authority or a better job title? Not, what can I do for *me*? The only question that really matters is this: How can I help *you* today?"

Biff and Joe would constantly elaborate on all of this as the season progressed.

"Because in case you haven't noticed yet, we're training you to be different," Biff said. "If we lose every game of the year, go oh-and-ten on the football field, as long as we try hard, I don't care. You learn these lessons, and we're ten- and-oh in the game of life."

One of my favorite afternoon talks was based on a Bible story—the parable of talents—that Joe had recently shared with Biff. The story comes from the Book of Matthew.

It begins with a man who was preparing to leave home on a journey. He called his servants and distributed his property to them based on ability. To one servant he gave five talents—a talent being a monetary unit that was more than the total wages a laborer would earn in fifteen years. To another servant the man gave two talents. To a third he gave only one. Then the man left. The servants were on their own. As the story goes: "He who had received the five talents went at once and traded with them; and he made five talents more. So also, he who had the two talents made two talents more. But he who had received the one talent went and dug in the ground and hid his master's money." Eventually, the master returned to settle accounts with his servants. He was quite pleased with the two who had taken their talents and put them to good use. To each he said: "Well done . . . enter into the joy of your master." The man was not nearly as kind to the servant who had hidden his talent in the ground, making no use of it at all. Now labeled "the worthless servant," he was sent away "into the outer darkness" where "men will weep and gnash their teeth."

As Joe explained it, the message of the parable was simple.

"God gives each person X amount of talents," he said. "The question isn't really how many talents you've been given. That's the sovereignty of God. The real question is what you do with the ones you have."

Joe and Biff wanted to foster a community in which every member of the team would bring all his talents all the time—no matter what the number—and everyone would be welcomed as an equal.

"Some of us get paralyzed when we feel we don't have 'as much as' or 'as good as' someone else," Joe said. "But the person we really want to honor is the one who maximizes whatever it is he has. On the other hand, someone with great ability but without the work ethic and the right contributions to the team is really negligible to the community."

Biff played a numbers game with the boys.

"The world will tell you that having ten talents is always better than having seven, and seven is always better than five," he said. "Isn't that what the world would tell you?"

A few of the boys responded affirmatively. The others remained silent.

"Well, that's a *lie*," Biff said. "If a guy has ten and brings ten every day, that's pretty good. If you have two and you bring two every day, that's just as good. Do you believe that? Honestly, do you believe that?"

Before anyone could answer, Biff declared: "I do. The two-and-two guy is every bit as important as the guy who has ten and brings ten. Because the guy that has two and brings two, he's giving everything he has. What more could we possibly ask of him?"

Now everyone in the room knew exactly why Biff would never cut a player based on the level of his athletic ability. He would not hesitate to run off or at least temporarily suspend someone for drinking beer or mistreating a girl. Those were violations of sacrosanct team rules. But nobody would ever be cut based on athletic ability.

"Schools all over the country are cutting boys right now and sending them home," Biff said. "We don't believe in that. And I'll take it a step further. If you're one of us, which all of you are, then you're going to play. I don't mean just at the end of a game when the score is forty-two to nothing and it's mop-up time. You will all play in the first half of every game. It might be only one play, might be a few plays, but you *will* be in there when the game is on the line."

Why?

Because such a policy puts a guy with two talents right beside a guy with ten. As long as each is bringing everything he has, it validates that they are equals.

The first scrimmage against another team was on a Saturday morning at Gilman. This was also the first time the Grey-hounds moved up from the practice field in the woods to the game field right behind the main school building. They played host to Cardinal Gibbons High School.

While the Gilman captains huddled the squad for final words of encouragement before drills that would precede the full-scale scrimmage, Biff convened the coaching staff at midfield. He did not say anything about blocking or tackling or strategy. All he said was: "Remember, teach 'em, love 'em, let 'em have a good experience."

Gilman went on to outplay and outscore Cardinal Gibbons. That pleased the scattered partisans cheering from the modest stands—actually slabs of concrete built into a hill—on the home side of the field.

What really stuck out, though, was something Biff later said to one of the Gilman mothers. At a cookout after the scrimmage—family members included—this woman casually asked Biff how things were looking for the team. How successful did he think the boys were going to be?

"I have no idea," Biff said. "Won't really know for twenty years."

"Huh?"

She had been inquiring about the season. *This* season. Biff was perfectly clear on that. But he was not trying to be cute with his response; he was trying to make a point.

"I won't really know how successful they're gonna be till they come back to visit in twenty years," Biff said. "Then I'll be able to see what kind of husbands they are. I'll be able to see what kind of fathers they are. I'll see what they're doing in the community."

The mother managed to smile and get out something

about how nice that was. But she still looked somewhat perplexed when she politely excused herself to go sit with her son.

The first real game of the season would be played at night. That was the stated reason for conducting a night practice the last week of August—so the boys could get a feel for playing under the lights. But Joe and Biff had something else in mind as well.

Doughnuts.

"Big tradition," Joe told me. "Whatever you do, you don't want to miss the doughnuts."

I had already been around Joe and Biff more than enough to know them as refined experts on all things sweet—the Siskel and Ebert of desserts. They did not only eat, they savored. They also debated. With cookies, cake, pie, or ice cream on the table, Joe and Biff turned to serious analysis and rankings. I once listened to them go back and forth for a good fifteen minutes in a battle of the brands: Who packages better junk foods—Hostess or Tastykake? There was no clear winner. Another time, I saw Biff react with sheer horror when Joe committed the unthinkable act of declining a giant chocolate creme cookie from a popular Baltimore bakery. "Man, I feel like calling for taste bud abuse," Biff said.

Nobody would have to make such a call that night the team practiced under the lights. Once the footballs were packed away, the boys, still wearing football pants and cleats, boarded two yellow school buses. As tradition dictated, Siskel and Ebert were taking them to eat doughnuts at Krispy Kreme.

"Now, this is Gilman football," Biff shouted from a front seat in the first bus. "And you're all gonna wear those silly Krispy Kreme hats, too. Gotta wear the hats. It's part of the whole karma."

Biff was so excited he could hardly contain himself. Joe just sat back and smiled.

The guy behind the counter was a bit stunned when one of the assistant coaches put in the order. Customers don't generally buy thirty dozen doughnuts at a time.

It was almost ten o'clock on a late-summer night. Most high school boys in America were doing other things. The Gilman football players were eating doughnuts in a parking lot, chowing them down as if they had not eaten all day, and they were having a blast. The highlight had to be Biff donning his baker's hat and marching around to make sure everyone else was putting one on, too.

"Coach, maybe you need to get a job here," suggested Luke Wilson, one of the biggest boys on the team, an outgoing, fun-loving junior with a sharp wit to go along with some pretty good moves as a defensive lineman.

"Yeah, you might be right," Biff said.

There was lots of laughter in those buses. Lots of togetherness, too.

Chapter Nine

FOUR HOURS BEFORE THE SEASON OPENER—JUST AS they would do four hours before each game—the Gilman players and coaches filed into their meeting room for chapel. I never knew why they called it that on game days. Other than the addition of fresh bagels and orange juice for the boys, it was really no different from the standard afternoon talks Biff gave during two-a-days. It was still Building Men for Others 101.

The only change was the immediate sense of purpose, the intensity, showing on the boys' faces as they settled into their routine. Of course, they were still teenagers, so pretty much anything could set them off on a burst of silliness. But any clowning around would never last long this close to game time, and especially now, as the Greyhounds were preparing for battle against the DeMatha Stags, a perennial powerhouse team from Hyattsville, Maryland, just outside Washington.

Nobody could remember the last time that teams ranked one and two in the state went head to head in a season opener—if it had ever happened—and the drama was heightened by the fact that DeMatha was seeking revenge. The previous year, Gilman had pasted the only blemish on DeMatha's otherwise perfect season, a 14–0 shocker that made the Greyhounds the first team to shut out the Stags in Coach Bill McGregor's nineteen years at the helm. The 2001 season opener—seven o'clock on Friday night, August 31, at Homewood Field on the campus of Johns Hopkins University—was organized as a charity game to benefit the Children's Oncology Center at Hopkins. Two members of the Gilman football family had been treated there: Biff's son Jimmy, who was eight when he had a bone tumor removed; and Gilman junior Kareem Shaya, a team manager who lost most of his right leg to amputation required by cancer. Clearly, though, when it came time for the opening kickoff, helmets strapped on, adrenaline flowing, a few thousand fans whooping it up in the stands, this would never be mistaken for a charity telethon.

Once the boys were seated in the meeting room with their bagels and juice, Biff began chapel with a reminder about ignoring all the hype.

"Listen, this is gonna be fun, okay?" he said. "You're just a bunch of high school boys. This is a benefit game for some really sick kids. And that's all it is."

Win or lose, Biff played down the significance of the outcome. Regardless of the state rankings, this was still just an early season, non-league game. The main thing he wanted to see was good effort and sportsmanship.

"If we play our best, we're gonna run them off the field," Biff said, not in a cocky way, just being factual. "And when we beat them, I want you to have the same kind of class we had last year. I don't want guys taking their jerseys off and running all over the place. You know, be respectful."

And if DeMatha were to somehow come out ahead?

"I want you going straight over and shaking their hands," Biff said. "And remember, we've got a whole season left. This is nothing. It's not what you do now that matters. It's what you do in November. Okay? Our goal is to what?"

"Win the league and beat McDonogh," came the reply from all corners of the room.

"Win the league and beat McDonogh," Biff repeated.

Then he remembered one more thing he wanted to say about acting right on the field: "When we score . . . Ambrose Wooden, Napoleon Sykes, Malcolm Ruff, Stan White, Anthony Triplin, Mike Dowling . . ." That covered the top guns on offense. "When we score, please, guys, no dancing and hollering in the end zone, okay?"

"Especially Stan," Mike Dowling injected. "He's got *no* rhythm."

The room erupted with laughter.

Stan laughed right along. Poor guy. All he had going for him was chiseled features, excellent grades, tremendous athletic ability, and an engine that never seemed to run out of fuel. He was the most prolific receiver on offense and the leading tackler on defense. Schools all over the country, including his favorites, Ohio State and Stanford, were offering him full scholarships to play football. But not everyone was born to dance.

"No moves, man, none," Mike said of his fellow senior and co-captain.

Biff chuckled. Joe smiled. Both enjoyed being with Mike, a witty and driven young man who excelled in both academics—a longtime honor student—and athletics. More than anything, they were thrilled to see the way he had blossomed into such a reliable and likable leader. Mike was one of the hardest workers on the team. He was often the guy who yelled "huddle up" when someone needed to take charge on the practice field. Some of the younger boys trailed his every move like eager puppies. After everything Mike had been through, Joe and Biff could look at him now and see the value of their work, unmistakable proof that they were indeed changing lives.

Physically, Mike was a bruiser, six-foot-two, 235 heavy-duty pounds, with a massive chest and bulging biceps. In addition to being a top-notch football player—hard-hitting fullback on offense and linebacker on defense—Mike was also one of the best prep wrestlers in Maryland. Emotionally, however, he was not always so sturdy and sure of himself. Though in one sense a child of privilege—his parents were quite successful in real-estate management and Mike had never wanted for anything material—he was also a product of turmoil. His parents split when he was twelve, but that did not end the ugliness between them. Mike lived with his mother, Nancy, a doting and overindulgent parent, but he did not have much of a relationship with his father and sometimes felt terribly alone. Mike had an older brother to whom he might have turned for guidance and support, but J.T. was a bit of a loose cannon who partied more than the average teen and was expelled from Gilman when he was a junior. In an essay written as part of a college application, Mike would choose the words *turbulent* and *numbing* to describe his family life.

That lack of stability at home deeply concerned Joe and Biff when Mike brought on a little trouble of his own. It happened in the Gilman football camp during the summer of 2000. It was an aberration for Mike—and certainly a minor event in the big scheme of things—but it could have been devastating for him.

The whole episode started because Mike was upset with the way he was being used in practice. He was stuck on the offensive line instead of being played at fullback. And he was also concerned that he was being squeezed out of playing time at linebacker. When Mike privately shared his unhappiness with the coaching staff, Biff reminded him that he ought to be thinking only of what was best for the team. He also asked Mike to be patient and assured him that everything would ultimately work out the way it should. But Mike was unable to temper his frustration. Biff soon got the feeling that Mike was not always putting maximum effort into blocking at his guard position. Maybe it was a ploy to play himself out of his unwanted spot on the offensive line. One day at practice, Biff made the offense rerun a play because he thought Mike had not tried hard enough. When the play was repeated, Biff thought Mike was still holding back, and he once again halted the action to get after him about it.

"I'm trying my best," Mike exploded. "I don't need this shit."

"What did you say?" Biff asked.

"I don't need this shit," Mike repeated.

"Get off the field."

"I'm not coming back."

"Get off the field!"

Storming away toward the field house, Mike immediately realized how wrong he had been. But it was too late to turn back. Biff would never tolerate such disrespect from a player. It was not only the outburst of profanity that angered and disappointed him. In a broader sense, it was also the matter of selfishness. It was the way Mike had persisted in putting his own agenda before the needs of the team. Biff discussed that with Joe, then with their senior captains, and the boys voted Mike off the team. No specific length of time was placed on his suspension. For the time being, though, one point was indisputable: Mike Dowling was no longer a Greyhound football player.

"I was crushed," he would later tell me. "I mean, all my best friends were on the team. I'd always been so into football. It gave me so much structure and continuity in my life. And now it was gone."

He felt guilty. He felt tainted. Sometimes he even felt sick, physically sick, about the whole thing. *I need to be with my friends,* Mike kept thinking. *They need me. And I need them.*

Mike apologized profusely for his outburst on the practice field. Biff and Joe were inclined to let him back on the team after sitting out the first game of the season. But then two other transgressions were brought to their attention. In what had started out as a playful exchange between friends, Mike had gone too far in the teasing of a teammate, almost leading to a fight. And, in a separate incident, he had angered another teammate by targeting him with a vile prank in the locker room. Clearly, Mike was not acting like a man built for others.

Forced to keep watching his teammates from the stands, Mike felt himself drowning in a sea of remorse. A month into the season, he once again appealed to Biff and Joe for reinstatement. This time he broke down in tears while explaining how badly he needed to be back with his friends, how desperately he wanted one more chance to embrace fully the concept of community. Biff and Joe confronted a concern with which they'd already struggled for weeks: Perhaps they were doing Mike more harm than good by keeping him away. After all, he was exactly the type of boy who needed their influence, and Building Men for Others was all about saving people, not casting them away.

Ultimately, Mike was welcomed back to the team for the second half of the season. He worked harder than he ever had . . . cherished all the relationships even more than before. By the end of his abbreviated junior season, Mike was one of the best fullbacks in the state. Several major colleges were interested in signing him to play football. And— most impressive—he was becoming a genuine leader. He was leading with both his words and his actions. Only months after voting him off the team altogether, his Gilman teammates elected him as a co-captain in advance of his senior year.

"What a huge lesson in grace for all of us, coaches and kids, an incredibly valuable lesson," Biff said. "In the end, it's not the mistakes you make that really matter. It's what you do with what you learn from those mistakes. And it's also how you respond to the mistakes of others."

Surrounded by all his football friends just hours before the big season opener against DeMatha, Mike Dowling was exactly where he wanted to be. He had already accepted a scholarship to play ball at Duke. But first he would have the good fortune to revel in the joy of one more season, a full season this time, with his favorite group of people in the world.

Once all the laughter over Stan White's alleged lack of dance moves subsided, Biff pulled out a *Washington Post* story I had seen that morning and shown to him and Joe before chapel. I thought they'd get a kick out of one particular quote because it presented a philosophy so diametrically opposed to everything they believed and taught. I hadn't intended for Biff to use the story with the team. But apparently it struck a chord.

The article described how football players and coaches across the country had been "pushing the limits on every level"—high school through the pros—throughout the worst heat of summer training sessions. An alarming number of players had already paid the ultimate price for their efforts. The deaths of Minnesota Vikings offensive lineman Korey Stringer and Northwestern University defensive back

Rashidi Wheeler had been receiving the most national media coverage. But the front-page *Post* story cited the recent deaths of eleven football players. Some were caused by heatstroke. Others were linked to ailments such as heart defects and asthma.

"Despite the deaths, players are still willing to go to extraordinary lengths to succeed, and coaches are still willing to push them to get there," the story said. It highlighted the startling example of Josh Lawson, a mammoth offensive lineman at the University of Virginia who routinely compensated for dramatic loss of fluids by hooking up to an intravenous line after practice—thirty-three IVs in all during a recent stretch of thirteen days. "It's all about being a man," Lawson was quoted as saying. "Being tough."

Then came the specific paragraph that made me clip the story for Joe and Biff.

"You have to be physically tough on them," Seneca Valley High School coach Terry Changuris was quoted as saying of the teenagers who played for him. "You have to push them to the brink and either they are going to break or they are going to stand up and be a man. That's how you change these young boys into being men."

Biff was beyond incredulous.

"We ought to get a lifetime contract to play against this guy," he scoffed. "We'd beat them every time we'd play, because he has no idea what he's talking about. You understand? Fifty boys together, fifty boys that love each other and that are well affirmed and well loved by their coaches, will smack those guys anytime, in any*thing*. Being a father. Being a son. Being a football player. Being a doctor. Being an astronaut. Being a human being. Being anything.

"That's *not* how you become a man. Do you understand me? Because that means to be a man, you gotta somehow be some big, strong, physical person. And that's got nothing to do with it. Trust me."

Biff was so worked up, he just stopped speaking.

Joe stood up and started handing out copies of a worksheet he had prepared for the boys. It outlined the main topic for the first Gilman football chapel of the season—a Bible story about a blind beggar named Bartimaeus. It comes from the Book of Mark.

"Awesome story," Biff said. "I don't want you to think of this as some Christian kind of doctrine. Actually, this is a story about a bunch of Hebrews, a bunch of Jewish men who were together. Jesus was out with his buddies, and they were doing all kinds of stuff. They were healing people and teaching them. And then they came to the town of Jericho."

The boys had the rest of the story on their worksheets:

As Jesus and his disciples, together with a large crowd, were leaving the city, a blind man, Bartimaeus (that is, the Son of Timaeus), was sitting by the roadside begging. When he heard that it was Jesus of Nazareth, he began to shout, "Jesus, Son of David, have mercy on me!" Many rebuked him and told him to be quiet, but he shouted all the more, "Son of David, have mercy on me!" Jesus stopped and said, "Call him." So they called to the blind man, "Cheer up! On your feet! He's calling you." Throwing his cloak aside, he jumped to his feet and came to Jesus. "What do you want me to do for you?" Jesus asked him. The blind man said, "Rabbi, I want to see." "Go," said Jesus, "your faith has healed you." Immediately he received his sight and followed Jesus along the road.

"See, in my way of reading this, this is a story about today as much as it was a story about two thousand years ago,"

Biff said. "Because it's a story about social divisions. It's a story about boxes and separations. It's a story about *isms*, isn't it? Social*isms* and physical*isms* and class*isms*. This whole story—how Bartimaeus was treated—was based on one thing. His outward appearance. His physical characteristics. Nowhere in there do they tell you anything about what kind of personality he had, what kind of heart he had, any of that, do they? What do they tell you about what kind of person he was?"

"Blind man," said junior Victor Abiamiri, a six-foot-five man-child who was by far the most talented and dominant player on both the offensive and defensive lines. The first day of practice, Joe had pointed him out to me as the one Gilman guy most likely to end up playing in the NFL.

"He's a *blind . . . beggar*," Biff said, pushing out those last two words as if they were toxic. "So because of that the people have made all kinds of judgments about Bartimaeus. Think of that. And they put him in a bunch of boxes. We do it all the time. We look at a guy, the color of his skin, we put him in a box. Look at his body type, put him in a box. The diploma he has, put him in a box. Where he lives, car he drives, put him in a box. Right? Don't we? Girl he dates, clothes he wears, put him in a box."

In the language of Building Men for Others, Biff said, the crowd simply refused to empathize with Bartimaeus.

"All he asked for was mercy," Biff said. "There's no pretension in that plea, is there? It's the last thing you ask for when you're just down and out and crushed. *Mercy*. They couldn't even give him that. They rebuked him when he spoke out. They were embarrassed by him. Because they were so focused on themselves—the *opposite* of empathy."

Ultimately, Biff said, Bartimaeus got what he needed, both mercy and sight, only because Jesus looked at him as someone who mattered, and he asked one simple but powerful question: "What do you want me to do for you?" It was basically the same question Biff and Joe had already introduced as the guiding force behind a man built for others: What can *I* do for *you*?

There was one other element of this story—the significance of the name Bartimaeus—that would stay fresh in my mind long after chapel and the game against DeMatha. It stuck with me because it made me think about my father.

"Coach Ehrmann taught me this," Biff said. "Bar, b-a-r, in Hebrew means *son of*. So when we have a bar mitzvah"— the Jewish ritual marking a boy's thirteenth birthday and celebrating him as one who is responsible for the Commandments—"that's a ceremony that means you now become son of the law. Well, *Bar*timaeus, he was the son of Timaeus. The writer even makes a point of saying it, the son of Timaeus. Now, there are all kinds of stories throughout the Bible, there's the poor guy, there's the widow, there's the orphan, but they don't name them. In this one, they name him. *Bar*timaeus. *Son of*. He's some dad's boy, right?"

Biff and Joe often made the point that every boy is "some mom's boy" and therefore "the most precious thing" in that woman's life. That alone makes every boy special.

"Well, Bartimaeus is the most precious thing in Timaeus's life," Biff said. "He's his *boy*." Biff temporarily shifted gears, speaking now as Timaeus: "Don't tell my boy to be quiet. Don't push my blind boy, *my* boy, aside. Don't treat *my* boy like an outcast. Don't judge my boy. He's *my* boy."

While the crowd failed to treat Bartimaeus as "some dad's boy," Biff said, Jesus was immediately willing to embrace him on that singular basis.

Some dad's boy.

I had already been thinking quite a bit about my father. Ever since Joe's speech at the University of Maryland—since I first heard him talk about his concept of the relationships that make a real man—I'd been thinking about my father and our relationship. Every now and then, Joe's words would start playing in my mind, like an echo on some kind of mission: "It's gonna come down to this. What kind of father were you? What kind of husband were you? What kind of son were you? What kind of brother were you? What kind of friend were you?"

No matter how many times I heard that relentless echo, no matter how many times I silently went through that checklist of questions without ever telling anyone about it, I kept coming back to my father. But this was hardly the time to dwell on that. With Biff wrapping up chapel, it was time to have some fun. It was almost time for football.

Soon after the Gilman buses arrived at Hopkins, Joe gave his talk to the boys about making sure to enjoy what would certainly be one of the greatest experiences of their young lives.

"What's our job as coaches?" Joe asked.

"To love us," the boys yelled back.

"What's your job?"

"To love each other."

As things turned out, even with all that loving, the Gilman Greyhounds were unable to put the ball in the end zone. Biff did not need to worry about any celebratory dancing. His boys were simply overmatched by a bigger, stronger, faster team. Gilman did well to hold its own after a first half in which DeMatha moved the ball with ease. But the outcome was clearly determined when the game was ended early—after three quarters—because of lightning.

Final score: DeMatha 16, Gilman 0.

It was almost the mirror image of a year earlier. So much for Gilman being number one in the state. Now that distinction would belong to DeMatha. The Gilman boys offered congratulatory handshakes to their opponents. Then they went home bruised—both physically and emotionally.

Chapter Ten

In addition to Gilman football, there was another element of my season with Joe: a series of one-on-one conversations about what it means to be a man. The purpose was to learn as much as I could about the unique framework Joe had developed. We worked from a list of topics I'd pulled from an outline Joe often used when he spoke publicly about Building Men for Others:

False masculinity
The relationships that make a real man
Working for a transcendent cause
Accepting responsibility
Leading courageously
Enacting justice on behalf of others
Empathy

Every week or two, we selected one of those topics and set a time to meet in Joe's church office. Though spacious enough for a corporate executive, it easily could have been the workplace of an associate professor or a struggling writer. The furniture—cluttered desk, rectangular conference table, small sofa—was modest. More than anything else, the room was filled with books, lots of books, most of them organized by subject. A wall of shelves behind the desk served as the theological library. Another wall was filled with literature on the study of boys and men. A third was devoted to social issues. There was one other visual—if that can be said of something noted only for its absence— that struck me right away. I did not see a single religious icon, no cross or wooden Jesus mounted on a wall, no paintings of scenes from the Bible. This was consistent with the overall look and feel of Grace Fellowship Church. Located just north of the Baltimore Beltway in the suburb of Timonium, its white, single-story shell had much more in common with the generic exterior of a giant mattress warehouse than it did with, say, Saint Patrick's Cathedral. Clearly, outward appearance was not top priority for the four thousand members of this independent, nondenominational Christian church.

Of course, that suited Joe. The Wednesday morning after Gilman's season-opening loss, I found him at his desk, wearing jeans and a blue polo shirt. After exchanging small talk and securing Diet Cokes, we settled down diagonally opposite each other at the conference table. Our first subject was false masculinity. Joe began by pointing out an incomplete message most boys get at the outset of their journey to manhood.

"As young boys, we're told to be men, or to act like men," he said. "Once you start getting close to adolescence, you get that verbalized pretty quickly. But the problem is that in this society, in most homes, it's never defined. We've got all these parents saying 'be a man' to boys that have no concept of what that means. Most of the fathers don't have any grip on a definition, so how could the sons possibly know what's expected of them?"

Joe told me about a simple exercise he often uses when directing men's workshops. He hands out note cards and asks the participants to write a definition of masculinity. "Most men are absolutely dumbfounded by the question,"

Joe said. "They really don't write anything at all. Or it ends up being a definition based on some kind of functional or material thing—getting a good job or something like that."

Sometimes he asks boys to answer the same question. "With kids, it is always about some kind of strength or power stuff," Joe said. "It's always about some kind of capacity to control. That's why it's so significant that 'my dad can beat up your dad.' You'll always hear young boys saying that to each other. To them, all that 'big, strong' stuff is being a man."

Returning to his original point, Joe said, "If you don't get some kind of a clear, compelling definition of masculinity at home, then you're pretty much left at the mercy of this society and the messages that are gonna speak to masculinity and manhood."

"Messages from where?" I asked.

"The movies, the media, athletics," Joe said. "I grew up in an era when John Wayne was kind of the ultimate man. Solitary. Lonely. Did heroic deeds but never was intimately connected with anyone. And then later you go from a John Wayne to a James Bond kind of guy. Suave and debonair. He has an awful lot of one-night stands. But there's no connectivity. And then you have all the sports heroes. As a boy, Mickey Mantle was kind of my hero, probably my first hero. With the sports piece, you constantly get all the glorified images of power and strength . . . the importance of being physical."

That brought us to the first component of false masculinity: athletic ability.

"I would say it begins on the playground in elementary school," Joe said. "I mean, you walk on the playground at recess, what is every boy doing? Either wrestling or playing some made-up game that has some kind of energy about me competing with you. Somehow it ends up that if you can hit the hanging curve in baseball or catch the down-and-out pass in football, then you immediately get elevated as being a little more masculine, a little bit better than the other boys. And the kids that can't do those things, they get deflated. An awful lot of a boy's value and the development of his psyche is built around that playground, probably more so than it is in the academic classroom. It's not near as cool to be the 'A' student as it is to be the kid that can score the most points. So that whole athletic thing becomes a dominant factor for just about any boy."

As boys get older, reaching puberty and navigating the treacherous emotional terrain of high school, they are deluged with all kinds of images and ideas concerning the second component of false masculinity: sexual conquest.

"It really becomes about girls," Joe said. "Sex becomes something that validates maturation and masculinity. So in our high schools today, it seems that the boys who can bring girls around them, who can manipulate and use girls for their own egos, for their own gratification, somehow those boys are being pointed to as what it means to be a man. As a boy who wants to be seen as a man, you gotta project that whole machismo kind of image, whether you're 'getting any action' with the girls or not. Because it's seen as kind of a shameful thing not to be."

Joe's third and final component of false masculinity— economic success—generally becomes a factor much later.

"As an adult, you start measuring masculinity, your whole value and worth as a man, based on job titles or bank accounts," Joe said. "Somehow it all gets tied to these concepts of power and possessions. And those that have the most are deemed in America as being real men."

Joe had a catchy way of summarizing our cultural progression of false masculinity—from ball field to bedroom to billfold.

"The problem with all this stuff is that it creates a paradigm that basically sets men up for tremendous failures in their lives," Joe said. "Because it gives us this concept that what we need to do as men is compare what we have and compete with others for what they have.

"As a young boy, I'm going to compare my athletic ability to yours and compete for whatever attention that brings. When I get older, I'm going to compare my girlfriend to yours and compete for whatever status I can acquire by being with the prettiest or the coolest or the best girl I can get. Ultimately, as adults, we compare bank accounts and job titles, houses and cars, and we compete for the amount of security and power that those represent. We will even compare our children and compete for some sense of fatherhood and significance attached to their achievements.

"We compare, we compete. That's all we ever do. It leaves most men feeling isolated and alone. And it destroys any concept of community."

Joe cited a staggering statistic from a study he had once read about: The typical male over the age of thirty-five has what psychologists would say is less than one genuine friend, not even one person, on average, with whom he can reveal his true self and share his deepest, most intimate thoughts.

"You really believe that?" I said.

"Absolutely," Joe said. "I see it and hear it all the time. The number one complaint I hear from most wives is, 'My husband has no relationships with other men.' Most women in marriages control all the friendships and make all the social plans. The men are dependent on their wives to promote and protect those relationships."

"Pretty depressing thought," I said. "Sounds a lot like the way my parents were, actually. I can't really think of any close friends my dad had on his own. And my mom was definitely the social director."

"Yeah, well, I just look at this church right here," Joe said. "I get to talk to most of the people on a pretty personal basis. The amount of pain men are in, and marriages are in—I mean, to me it's absolutely incredible."

"And a lot of that you trace back to your whole definition of false masculinity?"

"I do," Joe said. "Because there's no relational piece to it at all. All I can present to you is my facade. Here's what my external masculinity looks like. And I'll let you interface with this facade. But my biggest fear is that if you ever walk around this facade, if I ever let you in past my athletic accomplishments, past my sexual feats, past my economic successes, and I let you see this 'shamed' Joey Ehrmann . . . my sense is that you'll recognize me for who and what I really am . . . and you'll walk away. So therefore I'm not letting you in. We can still interact with each other. We can go to a baseball game together, go to the club together, watch movies together, talk about sexual exploits together, do things on some kind of economic basis together. But what I can't do is start talking about my sensitive side, my soft side."

"Where does that leave us?" I asked. "Where does it leave us as individual men? And where does that whole setup leave us as a society?"

"Isolated and alone," Joe said. "It ends up putting you in a situation where you're always hiding. You're always hiding who and what you really are. If you're hiding that, you really can't connect with anyone. Most men end up not even being able to connect with their wives. And then if you're not in any kind of community, and you're never sharing, never revealing who and what you are, I think that keeps you in a state of brokenness."

Maybe it was just that I hadn't gotten enough sleep the night before. But I felt the beginning of a headache—and I started to think it had something to do with the direction my conversation with Joe had taken. I was thinking about my father again. Joe's words were hitting way too close to home, my childhood home. *Never revealing anything. State of brokenness. A marriage in pain.* After years of unhappiness together—no outward fighting, all very controlled and well-hidden incompleteness—my mom and dad finally got divorced during my last year of college. Both eventually married again. Both seemed much more complete with their second spouses. But sitting in that office with Joe, involuntarily personalizing so much of what he was saying, I found myself temporarily stuck in the distant past.

I felt like I needed fresh air.

And we were only now getting to the really deep stuff.

It started with Joe telling me about an exercise he does to get men talking about their fathers. He asks them to list three words, quickly, that define their dads. Joe does this to get men thinking of their fathers not only as dads but also just as ordinary men with considerable imperfections and needs of their own.

"That's important," Joe said. "Because you've gotta understand, an awful lot of stuff that you got from your father—this is the case with any father and son—that wasn't about you. Me crying in the basement when my father was doing that whole boxing thing with me, that wasn't about me. That was about him. Crying as a six-year-old because my father was slapping me around and yelling at me? Pretty natural reaction for a kid that age. But, man, my dad had some issues. That's what I really had to learn and try to understand as I got older. I had to find a way to process all that. Because if you never do, then you're never gonna get healed. And then what happens? If I have my own son, then I'm gonna perpetuate a lot of the same things."

"The cycle goes on," I said.

"And if I'm not feeling good about my own masculinity, if I haven't taken care of my own business," Joe said, "then if you're my son, I'm gonna need you to be pretty masculine to validate *me*. And that's *always* wrong. Because no child should ever have to meet the needs of a parent. It should be strictly parents meeting the needs of children."

I never anticipated my dad having any role in this conversation. But now I shifted uneasily as I started explaining how much I'd been thinking about him the last few weeks.

"Hearing you talk about your father, reading some of the material you've given me, listening to you and Biff at practice, it's all got me thinking," I said. "As you said when we first got into this, it's gonna be a journey for both of us and who knows where it eventually takes us, but I think one of the things I'm going to end up doing is hopefully figuring out some things with my own father-son relationship. I used to think we had a great relationship, especially when I was younger. And it's not that we have a *bad* relationship by any means. It's just that we don't have the kind of connection that we used to have when I was younger."

"See, when you're younger," Joe said, "you almost have to believe you've got a great relationship. I thought I had this fabulous relationship with my father."

"Up until what point?" I said. "I mean, as a kid you felt that way?"

"Oh, yeah, my father was my hero."

"Even though he wasn't around much?"

"Even though he wasn't around much," Joe said. "You know, I loved him dearly. I loved him dearly. But I think all kids are going to champion or herald their fathers, whether they're around or not around, no matter how good or bad they are."

I did not want Joe to get the wrong idea. I explained that my dad had always been around for me. He had always been a good—extremely good—influence on me. It was just that certain things were never within the reach of our father-son dialogue.

I started backing into a personal story of my own by asking Joe: "When was the first time your father told you that he loved you? Was that something he said to you as a child?"

"Oh, never as a child," Joe said. "No, only as an adult. It was either at or right after my ordination. At the end of his life, I don't think I ever saw him when he didn't tell me he loved me."

"What brought that out finally?"

"I think his own healing."

I told Joe about the first time I heard "I love you" from my father. I was twenty-four. We were speaking by telephone one night toward the end of my stint as a reporter in Kentucky. Sitting on the couch in my apartment, I was shocked when he closed by saying, "I love you, Jeff." I responded, "Love you, too." And that was it. There were no bells, no whistles, no certificates to commemorate the occasion. I just hung up the phone and sat there in silence for a few minutes. Then the phone rang again. It was my sister, Wendy, then a college student. She wanted to tell me that Dad had just called her to share the big news. He'd been downright giddy. *Whoo-hooo! I just told Jeff I love him! How about that?* Wendy was happy for both Dad and me. She was also amused by the whole thing. He'd never said that to me before? And it was such a big deal that he had to call right away and tell her about it?

"Unbelievable," Wendy said to me. "Kinda huge for Dad, huh?"

Yes, it was. Pretty huge for me as well.

"That's a big moment," Joe said.

"Yeah," I said.

Unfortunately, though, it was much more a milestone than a stepping-stone.

We spoke more about my dad and our relationship. I did not want Joe to think for even one second that my dad was anything but an incredibly loving father—loving in his actions.

"But that doesn't mean there's not still some serious stuff there," I said.

"Yeah, well, if you really want to talk to him about it, really want to unpack all that stuff between the two of you, you just have to affirm him that it isn't some fault-finding thing," Joe said. "It's just to help you understand who you are and what you are."

"And what it really is more than anything is just a desire for improvement," I said. "Because he's sixty-eight years old. There are no guarantees in this world. This is not the kind of thing I want to sit around thinking about and then never have the chance to do."

Of the six guys I considered my closest friends—one from childhood, four from college, one I met later through business—four of them had already lost their dads and the other two had long been burdened by dysfunctional fathers now relegated to limited roles in their lives.

"I think an awful lot of men bury their fathers without

ever really knowing them," Joe said. "I always do a thing where I end up saying, 'Who was that masked man?' Kind of like the Lone Ranger. He kind of rode into the living room, did some heroic deed, and then he was gone. You know, I buried my father, I did the funeral, and it was three years before I had a tear. Took me three years to get any kind of emotion into it, which is quite sad. I don't go a *day* without telling my boys I love them."

Leaning back in my chair, I took a deep breath and dug a forefinger into my right temple, trying to rub away what had progressed to pounding. "You've literally given me a headache this morning," I told Joe. "Literally given me a headache."

Chapter Eleven

AS JOE AND BIFF SAW IT, THE ONLY WAY TO KEEP GETTING better as a football program was to keep upgrading the quality of their opponents. Gilman would always face the same schools during league play. But each year the coaches wanted to find new challenges beyond the standard part of the schedule. As Biff took great pride in reminding the boys before the second game of the 2001 season, "We will play any*one*, any*where*, any*time*."

That was precisely how the Gilman Greyhounds ended up spending the Friday evening of September 7 in the quaint, rural town of Ijamsville, Maryland. It was home to Urbana High School, winner of thirty-eight straight games and three consecutive state titles in the Class 2A division for small schools. All you had to do in Ijamsville was say two words—"The Streak"—and everyone knew you were talking about the Hawks of Urbana. If the Hawks could pull off one more perfect season, they would become the first Maryland team to win fifty straight games and four state titles in a row.

Of course, Gilman had other ideas.

The game was a back-and-forth battle right from the start. When Gilman opened the scoring with a thirty-eight-yard touchdown pass from quarterback Ambrose Wooden to wide receiver Anthony Triplin, it was the first time in two years that Urbana had even been behind in a game. With only four seconds left in the first half, Urbana finally scored

a touchdown of its own, but Victor Abiamiri blocked the
extra-point attempt and Gilman escaped with a 7–6 lead at
halftime.

The Greyhounds were playing much better than they
had the week before against DeMatha. But a few key mistakes—a penalty here, a fumble there—were keeping them
from knocking out the Hawks. Instead, Urbana took a 12–7
lead late in the third quarter. Gilman kept fighting, though,
and with less than two minutes remaining in the game, the
Greyhounds were in perfect position to ignite their season
by squeaking out a last-second, come-from-behind thriller.

They had first-and-goal just inside the ten-yard line.
Senior tailback Malcolm Ruff powered the ball down to the
four. But then he was stuffed on two straight running plays,
losing yardage back to the seven, so it all came down to one
final shot at the end zone. It was fourth-and-goal, fourth-
and-*game*, seven yards away from victory. The packed
Urbana side of the stadium—every man, woman, and child
fully aware that The Streak was in grave danger—went wild
in support of the home team. The Gilman side took more
of a hold-your-breath, wait-and-see approach as the players
lined up for the heart-pounding climax.

Ambrose Wooden took the snap and started back to
pass. Rolling out to his right, he was quickly pressured by a
swarming defense but was still able to lock in on Anthony
Triplin, who was waiting for the football just inside the
crowded end zone. Ambrose lofted the ball toward
Anthony. The ball floated . . . floated . . . Anthony was
reaching for it . . . and then . . . *bam*—an aggressive defender put an abrupt end to the whole thing by batting the ball
to the ground. Game over. The Streak was alive at thirty-
nine games (and Urbana would indeed go on to yet another perfect season). Meantime, highly touted Gilman, with

only a single scoring play in two straight losses, was off to its worst start in the five years that Biff and Joe had been at the helm.

The Gilman boys were terribly deflated.

Not Biff and Joe.

When they gathered the team at midfield, I expected post-game remarks similar to those I had heard the week before, maybe something about the boys needing to work harder in practice, something about cutting back on the mistakes, something about pulling together and making sure they start bringing all their talents. I heard none of that.

With his boys huddled around him, Biff treated them as though they had just handed him a world championship. He was that proud of their performance. They had played extremely hard. They had played with class. They had been part of a truly great game against a bunch of kids who had also played their tails off.

With both volume and energy turned up high, Biff told his team: "I wouldn't want to coach anybody in the world, *anybody*, other than you guys. I couldn't be prouder of a group of boys than I am of you. Look at me, boys. I love you. And I'm really proud of you. *Really* proud."

Nothing else was said. Biff and Joe just turned and walked away. That was when I witnessed one of my favorite scenes of the entire season. It was only a brief exchange between two players. But it offered powerful proof that the modeling of a man—in order to *be* a man, you need to *see* a man—can immediately and profoundly influence the thoughts and actions of a boy.

Ambrose Wooden and Mike Dowling were temporarily standing apart from the rest of the team, only a few yards away, but unmistakably alone. Sweaty and spent, they embraced the best they could while still wearing bulky shoulder pads. There was nothing extraordinary about that alone. They were the best of friends, and they'd just been through one heck of a battle together. But then I saw the tears rolling down their cheeks, and I heard what they were saying.

"I'm so proud of you, man," Mike told Ambrose.

"So proud of you, too," Ambrose said.

It was unimaginable to think that two high school boys would ever employ such language on their own. What teen-age boy tells another boy that he's *proud* of him? But hearing Biff put such emphasis on that word, having both the feeling and the communication of it modeled for them, had clearly given them license to express themselves that way.

When I later asked Mike about that exchange with Ambrose, he told me: "That was one of the most poignant moments I've ever had. Anytime you work so hard toward reaching a goal and then you fall just a little bit short, you can't help but feel like you failed. But you also feel so together with all the other guys. I knew that Ambrose would be really down. I was just reminding him how incredibly far we had all come together."

Ambrose told me: "That situation right after the game, I know I'll never forget that. It just explains my whole relationship with Mike. We're like two peas in a pod."

Imagine that. Two boys from totally opposite ends of the socio-economic spectrum—Ambrose an African-American raised by a single mother in a trouble-filled, working-class section of Northeast Baltimore, Mike a more-than-comfortable white kid from a well-appointed neighborhood in the suburb of Towson—peas in a pod.

That was the other reason that post-game scene made such a lasting impression on me. By representing the special friendship of those two boys, it also struck me as being entirely symbolic of the whole philosophy behind Building Men for Others. Ambrose and Mike were basically poster children for the underlying messages that relationships always matter more than anything else; that the content of a human being matters infinitely more than the wrapping; and that putting labels on people, making the mistake of treating people based on those labels, only extinguishes a plethora of possibilities.

When Mike spoke about "all the hardships" Ambrose had overcome, he did not mean the string of football injuries his friend had fought through. He was referring to much bigger issues . . . life issues.

Ambrose was in eighth grade when one of the Gilman assistant coaches first saw him playing in a youth football league and reported back to Biff and Joe that the kid had tremendous talent. When Biff went to see Ambrose and his mother, Robin Petty, about the possibility of Ambrose attending Gilman and playing football for the Greyhounds, he might as well have been talking about the boy jetting off to live in the Taj Mahal. That was how foreign and grand it all sounded to mother and son. And for good reason. Robin was out of work and did not even own a car. How could she possibly afford a private school for Ambrose?

Then there was the matter of academics. Financial aid could take care of tuition. But Ambrose, a product of less-than-stellar city schools up to that point, would first have to pass a rigorous entrance exam. After attending preparatory sessions at a Sylvan Learning Center and working diligently with a private tutor, he ultimately succeeded. But more than one skeptic remained in the Gilman administration. School officials insisted that Ambrose would have to repeat the eighth grade as a Gilman student. His mother was vehemently against it. But Ambrose finally convinced her that such a sacrifice was worth it to be accepted into their dream school. In the fall of 1998, he enrolled as an eighth grader at Gilman.

And now?

Ambrose was not only a football star with a growing pile of recruiting letters from major colleges. He was not only one of the most popular boys in all of Gilman, a magnetic blend of kindness and charm. He was also a dedicated student with wonderful results to show for his efforts. For the first quarter of his junior year—the quarter covering much of the 2001 football season—Ambrose would end up with an 89 average. It was the best he had ever done. His mother was so excited when she saw the report card, she immediately called Biff to share the good news. When Robin Petty, now an account analyst for an insurance company, uses the phrase "my angels," as she often does, she is talking about the Gilman football coaches.

"They treat Ambrose like a son," Robin told me. "It's like a dream come true."

The same could certainly be said of the many friendships Ambrose forged with schoolmates and teammates such as Mike Dowling.

"I knew I was coming to Gilman for my education and for football," Ambrose said. "But it's really the people—the people and the whole Building Men for Others thing—that changed me as a person. I think I've probably learned something from just about everyone here."

As Robin said: "It's rough raising a young black boy in the city—you know, all the drugs and the crime and everything else that goes with it. Now Ambrose sees another side of life. I wish every black kid in America could have this experience. The world would be a much better world."

Four days after the big Urbana game—the morning of Tuesday, September 11, 2001—I was in my bathroom shaving when I first heard the news over the radio. An airplane had crashed into one of the majestic Twin Towers of the World Trade Center in New York. Nobody really knew what that meant yet. Initial speculation focused on pilot error or equipment malfunction. But then came the urgent report that a second plane had just hit the other tower. That was when everyone knew we were in the middle of something horrific. The United States was under attack, the worst terrorist assaults in American history.

Wrapped in a towel, I hurried downstairs and turned on the television. Never before had I seen such panic and chaos—maybe in a movie, but not in real life. Firefighters, police officers, and other rescue workers were scurrying all over the place. No matter how many times the networks replayed video of the second hijacked airliner blasting into the south tower, the same unthinkable fireballs kept exploding and the same mammoth clouds of dense, black smoke kept billowing high above the southern end of Manhattan. The images were numbing. And this was only the beginning of a morning that will forever stand in infamy. Half an hour later, another airliner-turned-missile was intentionally flown into the Pentagon, just a few miles from where I was sitting in my living room on Capitol Hill. Then came three more shocking blows: the totally unexpected collapse of the World Trade Center's south tower, live on television; the crash of a fourth plane into the Pennsylvania countryside southeast of Pittsburgh; and, finally, the dramatic crumbling of the World Trade Center's north tower, also right before our eyes. In less than two hours of remarkably well orchestrated destruction, thousands of lives had been snuffed out and the national psyche had been severely jolted into turmoil.

Sirens screamed through my neighborhood as federal and local officials locked down the area to protect the Capitol, the Supreme Court, and other government buildings that could very well be targets for anyone wanting to strike at powerful symbols of our nation. With military helicopters and fighter aircraft prowling the sky, my feelings swung back and forth between comfort and fear. It was good to know we were being protected, yet the thunderous sounds of friendly patrols triggered breathless moments when I couldn't help but wonder if another air attack might be under way.

I spent the day inside, trapped in an emotional fog. Of everything I saw and heard on television, and I was glued to the nonstop news coverage late into the night, perhaps the most unforgettable image was described by New Yorkers who had watched in horror as people trapped high in the towers chose jumping to death rather than burning. As one witness described the sight of men and women leaping out of windows: "It was raining people." That alone pushed me to tears as I sat in solitude on my couch. Another witness added the detail that many of the jumpers had fallen in pairs: "People were holding hands and jumping." *Unbelievable,* I thought. *Only seconds to live, one final act remaining, and it was still all about relationships. Those people needed each other. We* all *need each other.*

Three long days later, President Bush spoke at Washington National Cathedral as part of a nationwide day of mourning, Congress voted to approve the use of military force in response to the terrorist attacks, and I returned to Gilman for the first time since the tragic events of September 11. It felt safe to be back on a football field with Joe, Biff, and the boys, a beautiful fall afternoon in the soothing sunshine, a wonderful respite from the palpable tension of the nation's capital.

During a break in practice, I spoke with Joe about some-thing I'd been unable to get off my mind—the people on the hijacked planes who had used cell phones to say their final goodbyes before crashing. In frantic calls to family and friends, all had shared three simple words they wanted to leave behind: I love you. I told Joe that I could not help but make a connection to our conversation about false mas-culinity. There had not been a single news account of any-one on those planes spending his final moments rehashing what a great athlete he'd been as a youngster, how many girls he'd scored as a teen, how much money and power he'd amassed as an adult. Nodding in agreement, Joe said, "Nobody was calling their brokers."

The next afternoon, Biff had a list of questions written on the board when the boys entered their meeting room for pre-game chapel.

> How will we act?
> What will we do?
> How will we respond?
> Will we lose our integrity?
> Will we lose our faith?
> Will we lose our humanity?

That evening, the Greyhounds went to Loch Raven High School and claimed their first victory of the season by dom-inating a thoroughly overmatched opponent. After the 48–14 rout, Biff happily told his boys: "Every guy brought all his talents. Isn't that fun?"

The boys whooped and hollered. It was a much simpler question than anything they had confronted in chapel.

Chapter Twelve

THE WEEK AFTER GILMAN'S FIRST VICTORY BROUGHT constant reminders that we were living in a new world. President Bush repeatedly stressed that the global war against terrorism would be long and difficult. Government officials warned about the likelihood of further attacks on American soil. Osama bin Laden became a household name. All of us—men, women, and children—were facing challenges we had never imagined.

What do we say to the boys? Joe and Biff wondered. They decided to build the next pre-game chapel around a simple message generally not associated with the young and strong: Life is hard.

At nine in the morning on Saturday, September 22, four hours before kickoff against St. Paul's in the first home game of the season, Biff wrote "The Journey" on the board in the team meeting room. Then he turned to face his players.

"What I want to talk about today, I think this applies to what we're going through as a country, to the times we're living in, to what's happening in our lives on a daily basis, and even to our season," Biff said. "I think this applies to all those areas. And the message here is that life is hard, boys. Nobody ever told me that when I was a kid, and I wish someone did. You know the first guy who ever told me that? Coach Ehrmann. It was in the course of about a year. My father died. My son had a bone tumor removed. A good friend committed suicide. Had a number of things happen,

and I was kind of caught off guard. *Life is hard.* It's a journey. And it's a good journey. But you're not always going to
be ten-and-oh. You're not always going to be carried off the
field of life as the big victors. You're not always going to rise
to the occasion. You're not always going to have everything
go your way."

That is all part of the journey, Biff said. And that is not
necessarily bad.

"Thinking about what's been going on in our world the
last two weeks, I don't think anything that's good is easy,"
he said. "I don't think anything really worthwhile is easy."

Biff offered an example.

"Every one of you is the most precious thing in the
world to your parents," he said. "Your mom loves you to
death. But what did she have to do to have you? They call it
labor. And having had four children, having been there
with my wife, I can tell you, it's *labor.* It's very, very painful.
But look what you get. You get *you.* And they wouldn't trade
those hours of labor for anything. I mean, they'd go
through that again right now to have you."

Biff shifted gears.

"Let's talk about freedom," he said. "All the biggest wars
in the world, biggest battles ever fought, were really fights
for freedom. You know, Hitler was marching through
Europe and just slaughtering people, six million Jews.
They're saying maybe six or seven thousand people died on
September 11. Think of six *million.* This country sent a
whole lot of guys to stop that. A *bunch* of guys gave their
lives over there. And you know who they were—the guys
that we sent? They were you. They were boys. Many of them
lied about their ages to go. I always thought: Why in the
world would anybody do that? What were they, *nuts?* And
then they bombed those buildings in New York. And I

understood. I understood. If they'd take forty-one-year-old fat guys, I'd go tomorrow. They went because it was right. But, boy, it was hard. Things that are worth it and important are *hard.*"

Biff discussed a broad spectrum of other things that are hard: being a good husband, being a good father, being a team player, being a servant by putting the interests and desires of others before your own. But of everything Biff talked about—all the hard things that define and elevate the journey—the topic that really grabbed me was integrity.

"Having integrity is hard," Biff said. "That word defines a lot of things—telling the truth, doing what's right, having honor. Mr. Finney used to use a word. You all know who Mr. Finney is? He's the guy this building is named after. He was the headmaster here for years . . . one of the truly great men on the planet. Mr. Finney used to say, 'I want you to have revolving integrity.' What does that mean? No matter which way you turn, or what situation you're in that turns you, people will see that you have the same integrity in every situation. You're not different here with me than you are tonight out with your friends. You're not different in class than you are at home. When a situation's easy, you're not different than when it's hard. Your character doesn't melt when things are on the line. You study the same for a quiz as you do for the SATs. You treat every person the same. You don't call a guy bad names when you're with all your friends, and then put your arm around him when you're not."

Joe had selected a story from the Book of Job that offers a dramatic example of revolving integrity. Job was a "blameless and upright" man who feared God and shunned evil. His tremendous wealth and possessions (seven thousand sheep, three thousand camels, many servants) made him the greatest of all people in his land—"the Bill Gates of his day," Biff told the boys. But then Satan targeted Job, killing his ten children, his servants, and his animals, all in an effort to show that sufficient provocation would turn even the most faithful of men against God. To the chagrin of Satan, Job responded to his flood of hardships with remarkable consistency. He shaved his head, fell to the ground, and worshipped God, saying: "Naked I came from my mother's womb, and naked I will depart. The Lord gave, and the Lord has taken away. May the name of the Lord be praised forever." Satan was not done trying, though. He afflicted Job with painful sores from the soles of his feet to the top of his head. Job was now so poor that all he could do was scrape his loathsome wounds with a piece of broken pottery as he sat in ashes. His wife said to him: "Are you still holding on to your integrity? Curse God, and die." But Job responded: "You are talking like a foolish woman. Shall we receive good at the hand of God, and shall we not receive evil?" No matter what his circumstances—blessed or cursed—Job refused to waver.

"Think about revolving integrity," Biff said. "And this is just the beginning for Job. We're gonna stay on this for a while."

That was it for now, though. The boys needed to get downstairs to their locker room. It was time to get dressed for football.

On a beautiful, sunny afternoon, Gilman took a 10–0 lead in the first half, but the Greyhounds were not playing very well. After winning in a blowout the previous week, they seemed to be stuck in cruise control against another inferior opponent. Joe and Biff felt that their boys were nonchalant, playing with a sense of entitlement, as if the St. Paul's boys would just roll over for them. Some of the Gilman players joked around on the sideline instead of paying attention to the game. Others committed senseless penalties and blew basic assignments on the field—obvious signs that they were not concentrating. Defensive line standout Victor Abiamiri, usually methodical and controlled as he ripped apart an offense, punctuated a sack by dancing in the middle of the field. To Biff, that single act represented the way the whole team was approaching the game—like a bunch of arrogant bullies who had no respect for their opponents.

Biff was furious.

"It wasn't about winning or losing a game," he would later tell me. "It was about the lack of effort, it was about attitude, and it all came back to something we're constantly trying to teach the boys. When you find yourself in a position of strength, a position of power or authority, you can go one way or the other. You can be a man built for others, which is all about effort and empathy. Or you can just walk around acting like you're better than everyone else, which is basically arrogance and indifference about the world around you. That was a key time for us. We had to decide what kind of guys we were going to be."

At halftime, the Gilman boys went up a hill between the football field and the main school building, sat on the ground in a secluded area, and waited for their coaches to speak. Nobody knew Biff was so upset, but it did not take long to figure out. He paced like a caged animal before finally gathering enough composure to address the team. Biff did not speak so much as he pelted the boys with his words. He shouted about the lack of intensity and about the penalties. He shouted about guys laughing on the sideline and about Victor dancing on the field.

"I am so *angry*, I can't even *tell* you," Biff screamed. He was so worked up—arms flailing, eyes dancing with fire, face crimson and taut—he looked like he was about to burst. The boys were stunned. Nobody made a sound or moved a muscle. In a closing fit of rage, Biff yanked off his Maui Jim designer sunglasses, mangled them in his hands, and smashed what was left of them to the ground. Then he turned away from the boys and stormed off toward the field.

Joe would have to clean up the mess Biff had left behind. But how? What could he possibly say to temper the severity of that tongue-lashing the boys had just received? Joe let the other assistant coaches speak first, and while they addressed what needed to be done in the second half, he appeared to be deep in thought. What would he say to make this all normal again, to make it acceptable that Biff had just acted so out of character?

Joe finally stood before the team.

"You know why Coach Poggi is so upset with you?" he began. "Because he really loves you."

Just like that—one simple question and answer—and Joe had the boys right back where he wanted them.

"Everything going on in the world, it's a beautiful day, you're young, healthy, and you're just not bringing your talents," Joe said. "It ain't right. Bring what you got, for crying out loud. Bring what you got, start playing like you love each other, and we'll have a great second half."

Biff showed up on the sideline sporting new sunglasses— "Had another pair in the car," he told me—and the Gilman boys finally started playing with passion.

When the game was over—Gilman 23, St. Paul's 7—Biff told the boys that he was very proud of the way they responded in the second half. He declared it a great "hump day" for the Greyhounds. They had gotten over a major obstacle together.

Standing in the afternoon sunshine with my new favorite football team, I could not help but think that it was also something of a hump day for me. I'd been so caught up in all the stress of September 11 and its aftermath, so depressed by it all, and this was the first time that I felt whole again, that I felt my usual energy and optimism. The world was no less harsh and chaotic just because I'd spent the day wrapped in the youth and innocence of Gilman football. But it was reaffirming to be part of such a special community. It was uplifting to feel the comfort and promise of something good.

Chapter Thirteen

THE NEXT TIME I WENT TO SEE JOE IN HIS OFFICE WAS the last Friday in September. It was a cool, crisp morning. Our topic was relationships.

With everything going on in the world—the FBI releasing names and photos of the nineteen suspected September 11 hijackers, Americans clamoring for a full-scale military response to the attacks, the United Nations adopting an aggressive anti-terrorism resolution—it seemed a bit strange to be settling down in a church office to talk about relationships. The more I thought about it, though, it seemed that our topic was not at all odd given the events of the day.

Joe agreed.

"What breeds terrorism?" he said. "It's relationally driven. It's hatred. It's prejudice. It's religious intolerance. It's racism. We live in a world that just *breeds* this stuff. And I think each of us has got to get back to some sense of the world that I live in, in *my* sphere of influence, how am I alleviating some of it? What am I doing to make a difference? Because we have the same kind of hatred throughout our own society, and all it does is spell death, man, whether it's death of dreams, death of hopes, or physical death."

Ultimately, Joe said, the building of relationships is really no different for an average guy striving to be a good man than it is for a world leader struggling with the causes and effects of terrorism. In both cases, strategic goals and consistent effort are required, and relationships work best when lubricated with affirmation and empathy. No matter what direction our conversation about relationships took, Joe somehow brought it back to the importance of empathy.

When we were discussing terrorism, he brought up the way his eleven-year-old son, Joey, had reacted that morning to seeing the names and photos of the alleged hijackers in the newspaper. "They're all *Muslims*," Joey had said with disdain. Joe had responded by reminding his son not to make the mistake of judging an entire group of people, a whole religion in this case, by the actions of a few. He had also suggested to Joey that he think about the way the vast majority of Muslims—all the peaceful, loving Muslims— must feel about the anger and hatred being directed at them only because they carry the same religious label as the relative few who were mass murderers. Joe had encouraged empathy—a word his children often heard—for all the "good" Muslims.

"Paula and I spend a lot of time teaching our kids empathy," Joe told me.

"How do you do that?" I asked.

"Oh, I think it's constantly asking questions," Joe said. "You know, somebody called so-and-so fat. 'How do you think that made that person feel? How's it feel when somebody calls *you* something you don't like? How's it feel when people aren't nice to *you*? How's it *feel*? Well, would you ever want to be responsible for doing that to somebody?' Another thing is when I read Scripture to my kids, when I'm teaching them, I read it from a point of empathy, always trying to understand the pain and suffering."

Joe called empathy "the single greatest trait of humanity that separates us from other animals."

I already had a solid understanding of what Joe called "false" masculinity—the societal-based, age-related progression from athletic ability to sexual conquest to economic success. Now I asked him to explain his notion of "strategic" masculinity—how he had come up with the term and what it meant to him. Joe started by talking about the influence a father has on a son.

"I think that there are three kinds of dads in this world," Joe said. "There are dads that are totally absent . . . no presence whatsoever. They're just gone. And the percentage of them in this country is staggering. The second kind is a dad that has presence, he's in the kid's life, he's in the home or he shows up at the school, but he doesn't deal with the more profound issues. They're the dads that invest time and money, and they care, but when they die it's kind of, 'Wow, I never really knew who my dad was.' And then the third kind is a strategic dad. He has a clear and compelling definition of masculinity and a code of conduct for being a man. He understands the importance of whatever transcendent cause he has in his life. It's strategic fatherhood . . . a clear definition and understanding of what it means to be a man and how a man lives."

"So it's strategic in the sense that it's something the father—or any man—has to actually think through," I said. "This is not something that just happens on its own."

"Right," Joe said. "It's intentional."

"Also pretty unusual, though, right?"

"Very unusual," Joe said. "As a dad, if you want to send a boy into the world with a sense of masculinity based on the importance of relationships, being a man built for others rather than a man living only for himself, then you really need to be there for him as a model and a teacher. But most men have no concept about any of this. They've never really thought about it."

"Which is sad," I said.

"Well, what we end up with is a cycle that keeps going," Joe said. "The father has no clue what it means to be a man, no strategic definition whatsoever. The son gets whatever the dad gives him. And so the whole thing keeps getting repeated. Without a definition, most of us don't even know whether we're good men or not. But most of us feel that whatever the criteria are, we're just below whatever that definition is."

I asked a hypothetical question: "If you could speak to every boy in the world—let's just pretend you could wipe out anything they've already seen or heard from their fathers or anybody else—how would you explain your own definition of what it means to be a man?"

"It's about relationships and a cause," Joe said. "Simple as that. What's a man created to do? He's created to be a son, a father, a husband, a brother, and so on. And all a man does is, he lives into those relationships. So I'm going to measure my masculinity—and it's really about my humanity—based on how successful I am as a husband. If I blow it there, or if I blow it as a dad, nothing else really matters. All the power and prestige and possessions in the world will never make up for failed relationships."

"How do you teach all this to someone?" I asked. "I mean, the boys at Gilman see it and live it because you and Biff are modeling it for them. But how do you reach people—boys and men beyond Gilman—on all this?"

"I think you try to speak into people's real lives," Joe said. "Some men just grab hold of it. Something I say might help them get connected to the pain in their lives. They might be ready for something new and different. But I don't ever know when it's really going to kick in for someone. I learned in the inner city with my work at The Door, I never really knew when those kids were getting the message. I've never known how to quantify it. But I do know this. It's really soul work. Something has to grab you in your soul. I don't think it's just cognitive."

Joe said that his painful memories and emotions related to his father were the only catalyst he had ever needed to make sure that he was giving his own sons a clear and consistent message about the importance of relationships and strategic masculinity.

"Most of us have a huge father pain somewhere deep down inside, a huge father longing," Joe said. "Because we have never been accepted, never been embraced the way we need to be. I just know when I touch the pain of my own father wound, I don't want my boys to have that."

Joe told me about a common condition—known to psychologists as normative male alexithymia—that goes a long way in explaining why many men struggle with relationships. The word *alexithymia* has Greek roots. It means the inability to put emotions into words. As described by psychologist Ronald F. Levant, who has written extensively on masculinity: "Normative alexithymia is a predictable result of the male gender role socialization process. Specifically, it is a result of boys being socialized to restrict the expression of their vulnerable and caring/connection emotions and to be emotionally stoic." Levant cites a significant amount of research showing that males actually begin life more emotionally expressive than females. Infant boys are more easily startled and excited, exhibit less tolerance for tension and frustration, cry sooner and more often, and change moods more rapidly than do infant girls. The socialization process takes hold with remarkable speed, though. By the age of two, boys are already showing verbal signs of tuning out and suppressing their emotions.

"Doesn't bode too well for what comes later," I said.

"No," Joe said. "If we can't even formulate words to speak about our emotions, that leaves us with tremendous problems when it comes to relationships and our ability to live in community. So we learn how to live in *pseudo*-community. We build walls. We fake relationships—because all you know is my facade, all I know is your facade. We end up isolated. And we end up living with that whole flawed paradigm we talked about last time you were here. We compare and we compete, but we never really *connect*."

"Sounds like men have to start talking more," I said.

"If I want to have authentic relationships, then I can't keep hiding and protecting myself," Joe said. "Somehow I've got to be able to let people in, and once I let them in, then and only then do I have a chance to really be loved. Then and only then do I have a chance to truly and totally share myself with others."

Joe took a call on his cell phone. It seemed that he would be a few minutes, so I got up and browsed through the books lining his shelves. I came across a little book Joe had recently told me about, called *Questions for My Father: Finding the Man Behind Your Dad*. The author, Vincent Staniforth, was thirty when his father died. It did not take Staniforth long to realize how much he had failed to discuss with his dad. The book is a collection of questions he will never get to ask.

"I had ample opportunity to ask Dad these questions when he was alive," Staniforth writes. "But it seemed that a million reasons not to do so could always be found. It was a waste of everything Dad had ever seen, done, and thought about not to hear his answers, and I regret not finding out more about him when I had the chance. *Questions for My Father* was born of that regret and has one underlying objective: to develop a blueprint for discovery so that children of any age can start to build a clearer, deeper picture of the man behind the word *Dad*."

I flipped through the pages and found lots of good questions. There were serious questions and whimsical questions—none of them in any particular order.

"What did you always want to do but never had the chance?"

"What do you believe happens when we die?"

"Do you think you're a contented man?"

"If you could change one thing about me, what would it be?"

"What was your first job?"

"What was the funniest thing you ever saw your children do?"

When Joe was done on the phone, he saw what I was reading and said: "I use that book all the time with my boys. Pretty simple stuff . . . and yet utterly profound."

"Mind if I borrow it?" I asked.

"Take it," Joe said.

Later that day, back in my office at home, I read the entire book, which did not take long. When I was done, I turned back to a brief passage about midway through the book: "How do you ask these questions without creating an awkward moment? Maybe that's the problem. We've gotten out of the habit of having meaningful conversations. One of the casualties of our time is that the people who should matter the most are the ones we often take for granted."

With that final thought still bouncing around in my mind, I closed *Questions for My Father* and added it to an ever-growing pile of books cluttering the floor in the back corner of my office.

Chapter Fourteen

SENIOR NAPOLEON SYKES, SON OF A CITY BUS DRIVER, youngest of three children, always brought a lot to Gilman football. He brought a load of talent and energy. The five-foot-nine, 180-pound wide receiver and defensive back once scored four touchdowns in a game—as a junior— before signing to play at Wake Forest. He brought leadership. Napoleon was often the last player to speak in the team huddle before the start of a game. He brought the sensitivity of a deep thinker. Writing poetry was one of his favorite things to do. He brought an appreciation of the fact that his high school football experience—specifically the Building Men for Others component—had forever changed him. "I have found a new definition of family," Napoleon had written in a letter to his coaches at the end of his sophomore season. "I realize now that family is more than just a word. I really understand it now."

The morning of Saturday, September 29, game day at home against Mount St. Joseph, Napoleon also brought to Gilman football something beyond his usual bundle of offerings. He brought the memory of his best friend. Ryan Smith had lived next door to Napoleon. A year younger, he was the little brother Napoleon had always wanted. They played basketball together under the streetlights. They turned silly arguments into fun-filled wrestling matches— always teasing each other and laughing endlessly. They also had each other to hash over their hopes and dreams. But then a drunken driver made an impossible left turn across traffic and put an end to all that. Had things gone differently the night of Saturday, December 2, 2000, had Ryan been anywhere but the intersection of Greenwich Avenue and Baltimore National Pike when thirty-seven-year-old Jean Marie Lynch was driving her Dodge Shadow with three and a half times the legal limit of alcohol in her blood, well, then he and Napoleon would now be preparing for one of the most enjoyable games of their lives. Ryan would be playing linebacker for Mount St. Joseph. Best friends would be competing for bragging rights.

On his way to Gilman for the fifth game of the year—midpoint of his final high school season—Napoleon did not want to dwell on lost possibilities. He just wanted to enjoy being with his football family, wanted to be like any other high school athlete lapping up the excitement of youth and competition. But he could never just wish away the memory of what happened to Ryan. Two months shy of his sixteenth birthday, Ryan was an outgoing boy who loved to spin records and wanted to pursue a career as a radio disk jockey. He was a big, strong kid, but he was not wearing a seat belt and never had a chance against the violent impact of the crash. The Ford Expedition in which he was riding—his brother DeMarco behind the wheel—rolled over and hit a light pole. Ryan suffered severe head wounds. Rescue workers pulled him from the wreckage and rushed him to Maryland Shock Trauma Center.

Napoleon did not find out until early the next morning. Hardly able to believe what he was hearing, he went straight to the hospital and found Ryan in the shadows of death. All sorts of machines were connected to him, blinking and beeping, pumping air in and out of his chest, draining fluids, but offering only temporary sustenance. Feeling a piece of himself dying right along with his friend, Napoleon did what came naturally. He called Biff.

"Coach, I'm going to need you here," Napoleon said. "And can you bring Coach Ehrmann?" Next thing Napoleon knew, Biff and Joe were there with him, hugging him, offering whatever comfort they could. In a cold, cramped room, they leaned over Ryan, gently rubbing his hands and forearms, and they whispered words of encouragement and love. They bowed their heads and Joe led them in prayer. Hours later, Ryan Smith was pronounced dead.

New Psalmist Baptist Church was jam-packed for the funeral, standing room only. Having been asked by Ryan's father to offer a eulogy, Napoleon stood over the open casket and spoke directly to his best friend.

"Hey, Ryan," he began. "What's up? Can you turn off the turntables and call back whomever you are talking to? I need to talk to you."

Napoleon told Ryan about some of the lessons his football coaches had taught him about being a man. The implication was clear: Though Ryan had lived only long enough to be called a boy, Napoleon wanted his friend to know that he had died a man. *Relationships.* All Napoleon had to do was look out at the countless people mourning young Ryan, just survey all the sad, empty eyes, and he could see the relationships that made a man.

"You were truly a masterpiece," Napoleon said to Ryan. "Just look at what you have done and how you have rubbed off on us. So don't worry about your family, little brother. We've got them covered."

Napoleon later wrote a poem—called "Losing Room"— to memorialize his final moments in the hospital with Ryan.

This room that shelters me from Nature's fury,
Built like none other I have been in before.
Fortified by one single wall,
And accompanied by three lifeless draping curtains.
A sharp breeze,
As if Death had breathed upon us,
Flew freely through this room,
Tucked away on the 4th floor.
It was December,
And yet the air-conditioner hummed,
Hummed a grievous tune,
Resembling a Negro Spiritual.
With my hand rested inside of his lifeless grip,
I long for the moment of impact,
Of his skin voluntarily squeezing mine,
Giving me a piece of my special gift,
That was rapidly fading into the light.
3 a.m. he is gone.

Walking into the team meeting room for chapel before the Mount St. Joseph game, Napoleon was even more eager than usual to strap on his helmet and make some big plays. He still had other friends who played for Mount St. Joseph. That was part of it. But he also thought about the coach who would be walking the opposite sideline. Napoleon had long been angered by his understanding—an incorrect understanding, I would later learn—that Mount St. Joseph coach Mike Working had not attended Ryan's funeral. Napoleon had not seen Working there, Ryan's parents and others he had asked about Working had not seen him in the church, and Napoleon had assumed the worst. He knew that Working and Ryan had never been close, but he still found it appalling that the coach would skip the funeral of a player. Napoleon's false conclusion served as motivation as he sat down with his teammates and started reading what Biff had written on the board for chapel.

The Decision.

A man . . . built for others.

A man . . . built for himself.

For those with no voice, no position, no privilege, no power, no authority, you be those things for them.

Seek justice.

Encourage the oppressed.

Defend the cause of the fatherless.

Plead the case of the widow.

The last four thoughts were lifted from the Book of Isaiah, one of Joe and Biff's favorite parts of the Bible.

Once the boys had picked up their bagels and orange juice, Biff told them to settle down in their seats. He started working from that outline on the board.

"Today's talk is called 'The Decision,'" Biff said. "And I guarantee you, all of you will have to make it at some point in your life. And the decision is a man . . . built for others. Or a man . . . built for himself."

He asked the boys to close their eyes for a minute.

"Keep 'em closed," Biff said. "Think about what happens in the world when people make the decision 'man built for himself.' Some of the great tragedies in the world happen when people make this decision."

Biff named some of them: "Greed happens. Businesses are run improperly. Young guys don't go to war to fight for freedom. They don't become policemen and firemen. Teams don't aspire to greatness. People don't bring all their talents. The quality of experience is eroded. Families break down. Husbands and wives go different ways. Children suffer. We can go on and on and on."

Instead, Biff shifted gears.

"What happens when you decide to be a man built for others?" he said. "You strap on the oxygen tank and start climbing stairs to save people in the World Trade Center. When you're the CEO of a company, you make sure everybody has a living wage, everybody has health insurance, everybody is treated with dignity and respect. When you're a high school football player, you play every single snap as hard as you can, with all your talents, because you play not only for yourself but for everybody. As a father, you make sure that you focus on what your children need. You make sure that there's no one, *ever*, treated better than the gal you marry. You do the things that you know you're supposed to do."

Biff told the boys to open their eyes.

He said that making the decision to be a man built for others really meant choosing to live by the guidelines espoused by the prophet Isaiah in that verse summarized on the board. Biff slowly read the words out loud, treating them with reverence: "Seek justice. Encourage the oppressed. Defend the cause of the fatherless. Plead the case of the widow." Biff said that those words were written on his father's tombstone—and that someday he also wanted them spelled out on his own.

"Not: 'His wallet was this big, he bought this many things, his football record was this, he had this kind of car,'" Biff said. "I don't want any of that. None of it."

Pointing to those last four lines on the board, Biff said, "I want *that*."

Out on the field during pre-game warmups, Biff made a point of checking in with Napoleon.

"How you feeling?" Biff asked.

"Pretty good," Napoleon said.

"You know, Ryan's watching over us now," Biff said.

"Definitely," Napoleon said. "No question."

Then the anger kicked in. Looking up at Biff, Napoleon said, "I can't stand Coach Working."

"Don't worry about Coach Working," Biff said. "You gotta do this for your buddy."

Napoleon thought he had his emotions under control. But then—as one of the team captains—he walked out to midfield for the coin toss. He was greeted by two Mount St. Joseph boys with whom he had served as pallbearers at Ryan's funeral. Napoleon had already seen J. J. Outlaw and Keon Lattimore a number of times since saying goodbye to their friend—Napoleon and J. J. were especially close—but now it was different. Already getting misty, Napoleon just about lost it when he saw an opposing player named P. J. Gilbert with a big number 5 on his jersey. That was Ryan's number.

In addition to playing offense and defense, Napoleon was the primary kick returner for the Greyhounds. Standing deep in Gilman territory to receive the opening kickoff, he was determined to get things started by busting a big run. But that would be hard to do with the tears blurring his vision. With the Mount St. Joseph kicker preparing to put his foot to the ball, Napoleon tried to wipe his brown eyes dry, but he couldn't get at them very well through the face mask on his helmet.

No problem, he told himself. *Time to get after it.*

Napoleon drifted under the kicked football, fielded it cleanly, and headed upfield behind a line of blockers. He got going pretty well, but the Mount St. Joseph boys took him down inside the thirty-yard line. It was time to play offense. But wait—Napoleon was not joining his team-mates in the huddle. He was slowly jogging toward the Gilman sideline. Was he injured? If so, nobody had noticed it when he was tackled. No, Napoleon was not hurt. He simply couldn't go on. He was too upset. His eyes were swamps. His cheeks were lined with tears.

Passing Biff on the sideline, Napoleon spoke as best he could through his tears: "Gotta get myself together, Coach."

Biff turned and followed Napoleon to the bench. Napoleon was weeping now.

"Ryan's with you," Biff said.

"I know," Napoleon said.

"Why don't you dedicate the game to him—play it for Ryan and his family?"

"That's what I'm doing," Napoleon said.

They kneeled to pray.

With his right arm draped across Napoleon's shoulder pads and jersey, Biff said: "Lord, please help this boy by releasing him from the pain and anger he is feeling. Please let him perform to the best of his abilities in memory of his friend."

A few minutes later, with the game scoreless and Gilman scrambling on defense, Napoleon stepped in front of a pass intended for his friend J. J. Outlaw and hauled in the foot-ball as his own. After scampering sixty-seven yards with the interception, Napoleon ran out of steam and was tackled five yards short of the end zone. But that was the play that set the tone for Gilman. Two plays later, the Greyhounds scored the first touchdown of the game and then they scored two more to hold a 21–7 lead at halftime.

Biff did not spend much of his halftime speech on foot-ball. He was much more interested in talking to the team about Napoleon and Ryan. For those who had not known

Ryan, Biff offered background. Then he explained what had happened with Napoleon at the beginning of the game. Biff told the team that he and Napoleon had prayed together by the bench, and that Napoleon had dedicated the game to Ryan and his family.

"Then what does he do?" Biff said with great excitement. "He goes out and breaks open the game for us! Now *that's* a man built for others."

The Gilman boys cheered with both friendship and respect for Napoleon. A joyous smile painted his face. Yes, Ryan would always be with him. So would his football family.

Gilman went on to a 35–14 victory. With the team gathered around Biff and Joe for post-game remarks, Biff presented Napoleon with a game ball. His teammates roared for him.

"Thanks, guys," Napoleon said. "Thanks for coming through for me."

"We love you," Victor Abiamiri said.

Then came a chorus of agreement from a number of the other boys: "We love you, man. We love you."

Chapter Fifteen

THE GREYHOUNDS BEGAN THE SECOND HALF OF THE season with a three-game winning streak and a bus ride to New York City. The stated purpose of the trip was to play undefeated Poly Prep of Brooklyn, ranked first in the state and eleventh in the country by *USA Today*. For the Gilman boys, the game offered a wonderful opportunity to make a splash on the national level. Joe was much more interested in the value of the trip itself.

"It doesn't really matter where we are going or what we end up doing there," he told me soon after we'd settled into seats on the first of two buses. "The important thing is just the going and the doing—the time we get to spend with the boys and the time they get to spend with each other."

In the five years that Biff and Joe had been running the Gilman football program, they had organized a variety of outings aimed at fostering relationships and building community. The annual visit to Krispy Kreme was only one example. There had also been pizza parties at Joe's house. There had been a Friday night visit to a local mall, all the boys wearing Gilman game jerseys, to see the movie *Remember the Titans*. There had even been a team outing to Baltimore's Lyric Opera House to see Mozart's *Don Giovanni* (no football jerseys that night). But this was the first overnight trip for the Greyhounds.

Joe had given considerable thought to the significance of such an excursion.

"I think it's important for the boys to see Biff and me in roles beyond the field, to see us being men in the outside world, not just authority figures who are always coaching and teaching and telling them what to do," Joe said. "And then there's also the whole 'adventure' piece to making a trip like this. There should always be some sense of adventure to being a boy, and this is really the best kind of experience a boy can have, because it's an adventure being done in community. When you're in a new place, new environment, the unfamiliar forces you to rely and depend on each other. So walls come down and we get a great sense of cohesiveness, a *one*ness. The boys will always remember this as a great adventure, and the relationships will always be tied into that. They'll always be right at the center of the memories."

With that in mind, Joe added, "Any trip is a great trip for the boys."

Though they lived only about three hours away by car, eight of the forty-eight Gilman players had never been to New York. To them, the oversized city was a magical place experienced only on television or in the movies. As senior Glenn Rivers described it: "Everything always looks so big, and everyone looks so busy all the time."

When the southern tip of Manhattan came into view through the bus windows, Biff showed the boys where the World Trade Center had stood for all but the last few weeks of their lives. The boys pondered their proximity to history. Biff also pointed out the Statue of Liberty. Then came a question from the back of the bus. "Hey, Coach, where's the Eiffel Tower?" Ambrose Wooden shouted. Yes, the boys would definitely learn a few things by staying in Manhattan and playing in Brooklyn.

They oohed and aahed at the vibrance of Times Square. They buzzed with excitement when they realized that our hotel was right around the corner from the theater in which David Letterman taped his television show. Soon after checking into their rooms, many of the boys rushed off to buy FDNY baseball caps and T-shirts to celebrate the Fire Department of New York.

Then it was time for dinner. After gathering in the hotel lobby, we walked a block up Broadway—one big, hungry throng of boys and men—to a modest diner at the corner of 55th Street. The location did not mean anything special to anyone else in the group. But standing on the sidewalk while waiting to be seated, I happened to look across the street and my eyes locked on the four large, metallic numbers identifying an office building that was intimately familiar to me: 1740 Broadway. I craned my neck to look for the signature star, an assortment of lights and colors indicating the time, temperature, and weather conditions, and there it was, still punctuating the top of the place. I was staring at the building in which my father had worked throughout my childhood. I thought back to the traditional Thanksgiving Day parades when my brother, my sister, and I would press our noses against the windows of our dad's office—five stories up—for an awesome bird's-eye view of the marching spectacle moving right to left down Broadway. There were lots of bands, floats, and giant balloons designed as Disney characters, and Santa Claus always brought up the rear, waving and *ho-ho-ho*ing his way downtown. The sights and sounds of the parade thrilled us. But part of the excitement was just being in that office. We loved playing with our dad's desktop calculator, or adding machine, or whatever that amazing gadget was called. Once the parade was over, we always got to sit with our parents and other families in the company cafeteria, sipping hot chocolate and eating powdered doughnuts.

"You all right?"

It was Joe, standing next to me on the sidewalk outside the diner. He had no idea why I seemed to be stuck in a trance.

"Oh, yeah, fine," I said. "Just having a moment, I guess."

"A moment?"

When I was done explaining, Joe said, "Great to have memories like that, huh?"

"Absolutely," I said.

I took one more look at the weather star. It blinked at me. Then I went inside to eat.

After dinner, we all went to see the hit musical *STOMP* at the Orpheum Theatre in the East Village. Returning up Eighth Avenue to our midtown hotel, the Gilman boys fell silent as our buses passed a fire station—Engine 54, Ladder 4, Battalion 9—that had lost fifteen men in the carnage of September 11. The front of the station had been transformed into a shrine, with countless flowers, candles, pictures, posters, letters, poems, American flags, and other assorted trinkets spilling out all over the place. A few firefighters wandered aimlessly in front of the building. They looked tired and maybe even a little lost—but not defeated. Definitely not defeated.

Looking at those firefighters amid the colorful tribute to their brethren, I could not help but think of the phrase *men built for others*—and I had to believe I was not the only one thinking of it.

Game day.

En route to Poly Prep, the Gilman boys were fascinated by the hundreds of Hasidic Jews they saw on the streets of Brooklyn, a collection of long beards and black outfits that was unlike anything most of them had ever encountered. Another valuable piece of the adventure, Joe said. The boys would always remember seeing something new like that, and Joe was always energized by the feeling that he was "broadening horizons," especially when the figurative expansion involved cultural diversity.

Soon after we got to the field, we were greeted by whipping winds and thick sheets of rain. "Gilman football weather," Biff shouted with glee. That was the clincher. After weeks of hearing Biff say the exact same thing whether it was ninety degrees with stifling humidity or a delicious seventy with gentle breezes, I finally realized that all playing conditions were ideal to him. It was *always* Gilman football weather. Biff took great pleasure whenever one of his players echoed his standard weather report: "Gilman football weather, Coach." Joe just smiled—a smile of both familiarity and amusement—whenever such an exchange took place.

This time, the day turned dry and even somewhat sunny as the players went through pre-game drills and the Poly Prep faithful filled the stands with the eager buzz of homecoming weekend. The game also marked a personal homecoming for Jon McGill, the amiable and decorous first-year Gilman headmaster who had moved to the Baltimore school after six years as a teacher and top administrator at Poly Prep. McGill was on the Gilman sideline for the one o'clock kickoff, enthusiastically encouraging his newly adopted Greyhounds, just as he usually did for a few minutes before making his way to the stands and cheering from there. What a battle he got to see between his former and current teams.

Malcolm Ruff got Gilman off to a quick start with a short touchdown run early in the first quarter. Poly Prep soon answered with a touchdown of its own and then jumped all over Gilman in the third quarter, scoring two more touchdowns for an 18–7 lead (after failing to convert two-point attempts following all three of its touchdowns). But the Greyhounds were not done. Ambrose Wooden scrambled in all directions from his quarterback position and a relentless ground attack allowed Gilman to stage an exciting comeback. With less than two minutes left in the game, Ambrose ran for a touchdown and then a two-point play, pulling Gilman within a field goal at 18–15. For a few seconds on the ensuing kickoff, the Greyhounds had an excellent chance to get the ball back when a short "squib" kick bounced beyond the reach of several Poly Prep players and ended up—ever so briefly—in the hands of Napoleon Sykes (or at least brushed up against them). Had Napoleon been able to field the ball cleanly, he would have had a clear path down the Gilman sideline toward the end zone and victory. But the ball went out of bounds off Napoleon's outstretched hands . . . and the referee ruled that he had never gained possession. It was one of several hotly contested calls on critical plays. But the football went to Poly Prep. So did the game—though not without one last flurry of controversy.

With Poly Prep running out the clock, its quarterback carefully gripping the snap from center and intending to take a knee to avoid any chance of a fumble, a Gilman defender dove over the offensive line toward him, a last-ditch attempt to strip the ball loose. The effort proved fruitless. But it did prompt a retaliatory shove by a member of the home team, and when Poly Prep was penalized for unsportsmanlike conduct, Coach Dino Mangiero stormed the field in protest. In his early forties, Mangiero was a burly man who had played defensive line for three NFL teams in the 1980s, and he was going ballistic, arms flailing, decibels rising. Once the referee had distanced himself from the tirade, he issued an announcement that stunned everyone on the Gilman sideline. He was ending the game without playing out the final minute. That made it Gilman's turn to challenge the officiating. It was not a pretty climax to an otherwise fine game contested by two highly competitive teams.

I'm sure that a good number of the Gilman boys will long remember every detail of that dramatic finish. But what I'll always remember more than anything else was the escalation of diatribe emanating from the opposite side of the field. It was not just the closing scene that brought out the fire in Mangiero. He was a screamer from beginning to end. All game long Mangiero had yelled at his own players, usually on the sideline, but sometimes bolting out a few steps onto the field between plays, positioning himself for maximum verbal assault against boys still in the game.

His closing act was the most upsetting to me. While his players were lining up to shake hands with the Gilman boys, Mangiero charged at them with instructions to abandon the standard post-game ritual.

"Don't shake hands," he bellowed. "Straight off the field."

In an impressive display of teen independence, the Poly Prep boys ignored their coach, sharing respectful handshakes and hugs with the Gilman boys. Meanwhile, Jon McGill, the bespectacled Gilman headmaster, made the mistake of trying to calm Mangiero, a man with whom he had long worked at Poly Prep.

"Stay out of it," Mangiero yelled at McGill. "You don't know football."

"Might not know football," McGill said. "But I do know courtesy."

The next f-word Mangiero fired at McGill was not football. I watched in disbelief as the raging coach cussed out the gentle administrator in full view of boys from both schools. Mangiero again reminded me of the same person I had thought about each time I'd seen him unleashing on one of his players during the game. It was my high school basketball coach, a similarly explosive and sometimes abusive man named Wilbur "Bil" Johnson, who went by "Doc," a reference to basketball legend Julius "Doctor J" Erving.

Doc was an athletic man who taught history and social studies at Blind Brook High School in suburban Rye Brook, New York. In his early thirties when I played for him, he was not exactly the buttoned-down type. His long, dark, 1970s hair was often pulled back in a ponytail. A full beard and mustache dominated his face. Doc was extremely bright and witty, had a very sarcastic sense of humor, and he was generally regarded as one of the coolest teachers in school. He taught me a lot both in the classroom and on the basketball court, and I thought the world of him when he was calm and reasonable. We had a strong bond. But that did nothing to ameliorate the fact that when he wrapped a whistle around his neck and took command of the gym, just about anything could happen. He certainly did not coach by affirmation. Doc slammed clipboards to the floor and screamed at us as if our failures to execute a play or win a game were affronts to his own manhood. Doc also went after referees. His temper was often on public display during games. But the most upsetting eruption came in practice one day during my senior year when Doc blew up at my best friend, Mike Woodrow, for throwing an ill-advised pass. Mike was captain of the team and our most talented player, small but solid and tough. He was also a fountain of sportsmanship and model of levelheadedness, one of the kindest and most respected boys in the school. But Doc was out of control, right up in Mike's face, concluding his rant with: "Woodrow, sometimes I just want to hit you." Mike stood his ground, chest out, arms by his sides, and returned the fury: "Go ahead, Doc, *hit me.*" Fortunately, he did not. Doc backed away and Mike stormed out of the gym. But it was an incident I knew I would never forget.

Watching the Poly Prep coach in action was not the first time Doc had come to my mind since I'd reconnected with Joe. I had already thought of Doc many times by way of contrast; he clearly represented the antithesis of Joe and Biff's coaching style. But the initial flashback came the day I went to see Joe speak to the football coaches at the University of Maryland clinic, when he used a simple exercise to initiate conversation about the impact men make on boys by either affirming or shaming them.

Joe directed his audience to a small circle printed in the Building Men for Others booklets he had distributed. The instruction above the circle read: "Write the names or initials of two men in your life through whom you felt affirmation as a boy." I wrote "J.E." for Joe Ehrmann and "J.S." for Jim Spano. Mr. Spano was a gym teacher and my basketball coach before Doc (seventh through tenth grades). He instilled in me a simple but powerful philosophy—"No Regrets"—that became the core of everything I wanted to be. In basketball, no regrets meant that as long as we did all we could to prepare, as long as we practiced and played as hard as we possibly could, then we would never have to worry about the outcome of a game. Win or lose, we would never have to experience the emptiness of regret because we would always know that we had given our best. But when Mr. Spano taught me about no regrets, he was not really teaching me basketball. He was teaching me life. He was teaching me that as long as I always expended maximum effort in whatever I was doing, as long as I always acted responsibly, as long as I always conducted myself with class and pride and extended kindness to others, then I would never have anything to worry about. *No Regrets*—that's what I'd want on *my* tombstone.

When the coaches were done putting initials in their circles, Joe asked them to move down the page to an empty square. The instruction read: "Write the initials of one man in your life who 'shamed' you and your masculinity." I wrote "B.J." for Bil Johnson—Doc.

Joe offered a hypothetical to the men sitting in that auditorium.

"Twenty years from now I'm gonna come back and do this clinic, and sitting in here will be the boys that you've coached, and I'm gonna take them through this same exercise," Joe said. "Do we want the kids that we coach to remember us in that circle—as someone who affirmed them, gave them a vision of what they could be, gave them some true criteria of what it means to be a man? Or would we ever want to be put in that *box* by any single boy that we coached, any boy that we've ever come across?"

Nobody needed to answer out loud.

Riding down the New Jersey Turnpike on our way back from Poly Prep, I pulled out a notepad and wrote a letter to Coach Mangiero. I told him about my high school basketball experience and about how much he reminded me of Doc. "That made me really sad for both you and the kids on your team," I wrote. "Sure, the kids will always cherish the victories you have collected. I still cherish my long-ago victories as well. But I left your field with the profoundly sad thought that your kids will inevitably, in the long run, remember you the same way I look back on my coach."

In closing, I asked Mangiero two questions.

"When you left the school, alone with your thoughts, were you proud of the way you behaved in front of so many people—most important, your own students?

"How would you feel years from now if you find out your players come to look back on you as I look back on my old coach?"

Mangiero's response soon arrived in my mail. He did not answer my questions. He did say that he found my letter to be very naive, ignorant, and insulting. He called me "an uninformed silly man" and asked me not to write him again.

Chapter Sixteen

A FEW DAYS AFTER WE GOT BACK FROM NEW YORK, JOE and I met in his office and talked about the second piece to his definition of strategic masculinity: the importance of having a cause beyond oneself.

It was a subject with which I was already quite familiar. Since 1989, when my then-twenty-two-year-old sister, Wendy, underwent a lifesaving liver transplant, I had spent much of my life promoting public awareness of the desperate need for organ donors. My volunteer work as co-founder and director of a foundation dedicated to that cause had long since eclipsed my writing career as far as the significance I attached to each. But I had never completely come to terms with that. I'd often heard gentle suggestions from friends and family members who thought that maybe I ought to spend more time writing—i.e., earning a living—and less time on organ donor projects. And they were probably right. So balance became the key. Even after years of trial and error, though, after numerous attempts at calibrating my priorities, I still struggled to find the right mix. For that reason alone, I was eager to hear what Joe had to say about having a cause.

He began with the same set of rhetorical questions he had been asking himself and others for almost a quarter of a century—ever since his brother died: Where do you find meaning? Where do you find value? Where do you find purpose?

"Somewhere there has to be some kind of a purpose behind why you were created, why you're living here, that transcends just who *you* are," Joe said. "You can't just go through this world about your own self-existence, self-concern, self-aggrandizement, all that kind of stuff."

Joe had a one-word description for such an approach to life: empty.

"I do a lot of funerals," Joe said. "And there's nothing sadder than doing a funeral when you have to manufacture something to say about the impact the person had in order to bring any kind of comfort to the family and friends. I hate doing funerals like that. And then in other situations, I find that no matter how tragic the death is, no matter how untimely, if that person had really connected to other people and also had a cause that touched the lives of others, then it's an easy funeral to do. No matter how much pain there is in that room, it's still a much easier funeral to do."

Perhaps that had something to do with Joe's notion that whenever we explore the concept of having a cause, we should always begin by contemplating the end.

"When I die, when I'm lying on my deathbed, what am I thinking?" Joe said. "Well, I'd like to be thinking that I've accomplished something during my time here. You know, I didn't die with the most toys. I didn't die with the most money. But I left something behind me. I had a cause. And my children, I know that they all learned the importance of having a cause."

Joe got up from the table at which we were sitting and grabbed a picture from its leaning position on a shelf behind his desk. It was a black-and-white he had printed from his computer the day before. His daughter Esther, just starting as a freshman at Drexel University in Philadelphia, a scholarship basketball player and psychol-

ogy major, had sent Joe the photo by e-mail. It showed
Esther—a tall, young woman in a dark Drexel sweatsuit,
light brown hair pulled back, blue eyes and teeth glisten-
ing in a gentle smile—sitting with a small, pale boy in her
lap, holding him around the waist. He was wearing a
Power Ranger costume and gripping a plastic sword with
both hands, but I was drawn to his eyes before anything
else. They were sad, tired eyes, and they were underlined by
a white mask covering his face from the bridge of his nose
down. The mask had nothing to do with the costume; it
was an everyday necessity to protect the boy from germs.
The four-year-old was fighting leukemia. Esther had met
him when her basketball team visited the Ronald
McDonald House in Philadelphia. There was so much for
Joe to see in that one picture. He saw a powerful connection to his own past: The Ronald McDonald House in
Philadelphia had long ago served as the model for the one
he'd dedicated to his brother in Baltimore. He also saw
painful memories—those vacant eyes, that mask—of the
struggle his brother Billy had endured while undergoing
chemotherapy. More than anything else, though, Joe saw
tangible confirmation of something he'd already known
for quite some time: Esther had an abundance of what he
called "the cause piece" in her.

Holding that shot of his daughter and the needy little
Power Ranger, staring down at it with great pride, Joe said:
"This gives value and weight to my life. It affirms me for my
belief system and my value system. It says that in the midst
of all my *stuff*, I'm making the world a better place. The
most powerful thing I can do is release four kids that are
filled with empathy, kids who can be touched by the pain
and plight of a four-year-old boy and his family. They all
have that cause piece, man, because it's been built into

them. It's been intentional . . . because Paula and I see that as being part of *our* cause."

Our conversation touched on a broad range of causes. We talked about large causes such as Joe's reform work within his church—always pushing his suburban colleagues to do more outreach programs with inner-city folks—and his development of a racial reconciliation project known as Mission Baltimore. We talked about small causes such as the way that Joe's thirteen-year-old son, Barney, back when he was in kindergarten, often took it upon himself to help a classmate who was confined to a wheelchair. Joe stressed that the size or reach of a cause was not the most important thing.

"When you have a cause, it should never be about trying to measure the so-called impact of what you are doing," he said. "It should never be about counting the number of families touched by your ministry, calculating the number of meals served at a homeless shelter, or whatever the case might be. Because once you start doing that, then you're right back to the whole thing being about *you*, focusing on what *you* are accomplishing, and it's not about you. It's about connecting to others, being *other*-centered."

I asked Joe to give me a scope of exactly what he meant—in his definition of masculinity—by the term *cause*. What qualifies?

"I guess it's a reason or a purpose to live," Joe said. "You know, why do you get up every day? I don't know whether it *justifies* your life, but it certainly gives meaning to your life. And it ought to define your day-to-day existence."

"So how do you go about finding a cause, the *right* cause?" I asked. "In your case, it all started with a very difficult life-changing event, Billy's illness and death. Maybe I had a similar experience with my sister and the obvious path toward working on organ donation. But aside from a personal experience like that, how do you find a cause? Do you just seek out a cause? Is it something that finds *you?* Is it a calling?"

Joe did not have any simple answers to those questions. He said that the first step—"part of the challenge of our culture"—is somehow breaking through and reaching beyond the compare-and-compete paradigm that leads to so much me-me-me thinking.

"How do you find a cause in a world where the value system gives you very little reason to even have a cause except when it's doing something for your own individualistic reasons and purposes?" Joe said. "Very difficult thing to do. I mean, look at the messages we're constantly getting. Look at all the media and marketing messages. We get all sorts of stuff about the whole mentality of always wanting bigger, better, more—the power of possessions—but that's only for ourselves. Where do we ever get media or marketing about wanting to do something for someone else, about having a cause beyond our own selfish needs, wants, and desires?"

"Certainly not the overwhelming theme," I said.

"So now we're back to the concept of empathy," Joe said. "To me, the number-one criterion for humanity has to be empathy. Without that, we're reduced to being nothing more than animals—you know, just self-preservation, power, issues like that. But when you have empathy, when you can understand the amount of suffering in this world, the pain that so many people are living in, and the causes of all that pain, then you can have a cause beyond yourself. I think the alleviation of pain is a fundamental root or seedbed for understanding some kind of cause."

Joe gave me a fact sheet—a list of statistics culled by the Children's Defense Fund—that he would soon distribute to the Gilman football team. If ever the boys required a reminder that someone always needed their help, that the alleviation of pain was always in high demand, this list, titled "Moments in America," could certainly serve that purpose.

Every ten seconds, a child is reported abused or neglected. Every thirty-two seconds, a child sees his or her parents divorce. Every thirty-six seconds, a child is born into poverty. Every minute, a child is born to a teen mother. Every three minutes, a child is arrested for drug abuse. Every twenty-three minutes, a child is wounded by gunfire.

The list had eighteen items. As troubling as they all were, the final item was simply chilling: Every four hours, a child commits suicide.

"Think about that," Joe said. "We are the richest nation in the history of the world, yet we generate a set of statistics like that. How can that possibly be?"

He answered his own question: "Indifference. The lack of being other-centered. Not enough people taking on any kind of a cause beyond themselves."

Joe reached across the table for his Bible—the first time he had done so during any of my visits to his office. He turned to the Book of Job and pointed to a highlighted passage in Chapter 29. "Now remember," Joe said, "this is the same guy Biff told the boys about when he introduced that whole concept of revolving integrity. Job lost all his wealth and possessions, all his children were killed, and then he struggled with his own health. His question now is: 'Why am I in so much pain?' His three best friends tell him that there must be sin in his life. But Job says no, there is not, and he gives this incredible defense of himself."

Job offers numerous reasons why he was generally well thought of by all who saw and knew him: *"I rescued the poor who cried for help and the fatherless who had none to assist him . . . I made the widow's heart sing . . . I was eyes to the blind and feet to the lame . . . I was a father to the needy . . . I took up the case of the stranger . . . I broke the fangs of the wicked and snatched the victims from their teeth."*

"Pretty impressive collection of causes," I said.

"Yeah, well, it's all about getting connected to other people, allowing them to live with dignity and status," Joe said. "It's never enough just to be sympathetic with the pain that others are feeling. You also have to understand what causes the pain, and then you have to do something about it. You have to figure out how you can make changes to help alleviate the pain. And, again, I think empathy has to be the key."

Chapter Seventeen

ONLY A MONTH AND A HALF AFTER SITTING PROUDLY atop the Maryland high school football rankings, the Gilman Greyhounds found themselves in a precarious position. With a mediocre record of three wins and three losses, their hopes for the season were teetering on the brink of extinction. The only performance-related goals they had set for themselves—win the league and beat McDonogh—could still be achieved with a strong showing in the final four games. But what had the Greyhounds really done so far that would foretell such an ideal outcome? In Baltimore football circles, the whispers were getting louder: After a stretch of four seasons during which Gilman had lost a total of only five games, this might be the time to get back at the Greyhounds, to beat up on them while they were down.

With league opponent Calvert Hall next on the schedule, there was a distinct feeling in the Gilman locker room that this was a pivotal time for the remainder of the season. As Mike Dowling said: "We either pack it in and head south, or we pull ourselves up by the bootstraps and keep pushing forward toward our goals." If the contemplation of such divergent paths was not motivation enough for the Greyhounds, this was also homecoming week at Gilman. The place would be packed with old friends and loyal followers. Due to a scheduling quirk that would put the Greyhounds on the road for the next three games, the Calvert Hall clash would also be the final home game of the season, an earlier-than-usual farewell appearance for the seniors. "Gotta get a win this week," the boys kept telling themselves. "We really need this one."

The Greyhounds exhibited what one of the offensive coaches called "a real sense of urgency" on the practice field. Joe had a different way to describe what he saw. Toward the end of a high-energy sequence of plays one day—lots of hustling and good hitting—he told the boys: "You're practicing like you really love each other. You're pushing each other, helping each other get better . . . finally practicing like you really love each other. It makes all the difference in the world. And it makes me really proud of you. Makes all of your coaches really proud of you."

Biff was also inspired by the hoopla of homecoming—and not only in terms of the game. Homecoming meant that the Gilman boys would party at a big dance Saturday night. That—along with the news that some kids had just been thrown out of another local school for alcohol violations—inspired Biff to structure his pre-game chapel around three absolute rules for everyone on the team.

No alcohol.

No drugs.

And you better not act like anything but a gentleman toward any girl you are dating.

None of this was new to the Greyhounds. They had heard it all before—to the point of redundancy. But sometimes repetition was warranted. The last thing Biff wanted was a phone call Sunday morning to notify him that one of his players had gotten in trouble.

Biff shared with the boys a simple but powerful observation that should be chiseled into stone at the entrance to every high school in America. He had never met anyone, never even heard of anyone, who said, "Boy, I'm really glad I got drunk, or did drugs, because I made a really good decision that I wouldn't have made without that."

Of course, Biff could not resist placing his three "zero tolerance" rules within the context of being a man built for others.

"You can't be the kind of young man I want you to be if you're treating girls poorly, you're sneaking drinks, and you're messing around with drugs," he said. "Because when you do those things, you're not thinking about anybody else. You're not thinking about your parents and what they want for you. You're not thinking about that girl and what her parents want for her. To be a man built for others, you *must* think of other people first. And I don't mean just during football season. I'm talking about every day, all day, all week, all month, every month, all year, every year— whether you're here or you're in college or you're off climbing a mountain somewhere."

As far as the Greyhounds were concerned, the last home game was also an unofficial Mother's Day, a special occasion to express their gratitude for all the love and support they had been given. A few minutes before the opening kickoff, the Gilman boys climbed into the stands behind their sideline and pinned corsages on their moms. The boys offered heartfelt refrains: *Thank you for everything. Love you.* There were hugs and kisses all around . . . lots of smiles and a smattering of tears lining the cheeks of proud parents.

Then it was time for the boys to show how hard they had worked all week. It did not take long. On the fourth play of the game, Ambrose Wooden took the snap from center and slithered to his right. He faked a handoff to Mike Dowling . . . and the defense bought into it. Mike was smothered by a defensive tackle and a linebacker. But Ambrose broke free with the ball—right through the hole created by the guys who went after Mike—and he rocketed past the Calvert Hall secondary for a seventy-four-yard touchdown. It was precisely the way Gilman had drawn up and practiced the play. It was also a sign of things to come. Sitting in the stands with a fragrant carnation pinned to her favorite Gilman football sweatshirt—the white one with "Ambrose's Mom" and "2" (his uniform number) stitched high on the left side of her chest—Robin Petty would have many opportunities to ring the cowbell she always brought to games.

Biff did not only celebrate the obvious offensive explosions and defensive stops that everyone saw. He also applauded the much more subtle restraint one of his players exhibited during an exchange that could have turned ugly. It happened in the second quarter, after Calvert Hall had already been penalized—unsportsmanlike conduct— for a late hit by one of its defenders. In response to that incident, Biff had marched a few yards onto the field and shouted to his offense: "That's not being a man. Walk away from that junk." Soon thereafter, Gilman senior John Lehr, playing right guard, had a decision to make. He was down on the ground, about to extricate himself from a pile of linemen after the action had been whistled dead, when one of the Calvert Hall players kicked him in the ribs. Angered by the blow and frustrated that apparently no referee had seen it, John jumped up and went face-to-face with the guy who had delivered the cheap shot. John glared at him. But then he turned and walked away without retaliating. While John joined his teammates in the huddle, Biff and offensive line coach David Payne showered him with praise from the sideline. At halftime, with Gilman leading 21–0, Biff had John stand up with him in front of the team. With his right arm draped around the boy's shoulders, he told everyone what had happened. "Every fiber in his body wanted to whack that guy back," Biff said. "But he thought of *us* first, the *team*. He knew that we needed him on the field more than he needed to be kicked out of the game for fighting. Now that's senior leadership! That's a man built for others!"

There was one other play, early in the second half, that registered with the Gilman boys as a milestone: a forty-seven-yard field goal by senior Tilghman Morton. Nobody usually cares a whole lot when a field goal is kicked by a team that is already ahead by three touchdowns. But this one was different. It sailed through the uprights with room to spare—a big-time boot for a high school kid—and it was something Tilghman had wanted all season. He wanted the satisfaction of knowing he could perform in a game with the same power and confidence he routinely displayed in practice. Forty-seven yards was the longest field goal Tilghman had ever made in a game. Maybe it was meaningless within the context of such a lopsided contest—Biff would soon pull most of his starters—but Tilghman felt the joy of a champion. His teammates hugged him and lifted him into the air as if he had just won the Super Bowl. At least he would not have to hear any silly quacking sounds out of them for a while.

The imitation duck calls had started—all in fun—in the aftermath of the absolute worst experience of Tilghman's playing days. In one of the biggest games of the previous season, on the road against powerhouse State College Area High School in Pennsylvania, the Greyhounds had gutted out a relentless drive down the field to put themselves in perfect position for a stunning come-from-behind victory in the final minute of play. All Tilghman had to do was make a thirty-one-yard field goal, well within his range, and the game would be Gilman's. But he missed. It was a wobbly effort—"a dying duck" in the parlance of football aficionados. Tilghman had never felt such overwhelming disappointment. More than anything else, he agonized over the feeling that he had let down the entire team. On the bus back to Baltimore, Tilghman buried his head in his hands and bathed himself in tears.

As time went on—Tilghman still down in the dumps about his mishap—two of his best friends on the team figured that maybe he needed a little good-natured ribbing to let him know that everything was really okay. That was how Mike Dowling and Napoleon Sykes came to perform a mock re-enactment of the infamous State College kick, not on a football field, but in the crowded common room of the main school building at Gilman. Napoleon kneeled down on the floor as the holder, just as he always held the ball for Tilghman during actual games. Mike played the role of Tilghman . . . and also took on the exaggerated tone of a broadcaster.

"Time is running out," Mike announced as he stood ready to boot a nonexistent ball out of Napoleon's imaginary grip. "Tilghman Morton is lining up for Gilman. Everything comes down to this. Here's the kick."

Mike swung his leg with feigned might. Then came an outburst of all the duck calls he and Napoleon could unleash before breaking down in laughter.

Quack. Quack. Quaaaack.

Tilghman just shook his head and laughed. The ice was broken. And the duck calls became a recurring gag. In fact,

Tilghman had even taken to assuming the duck role himself, occasionally sounding off with a loud quack or two of his own when Ambrose threw a shaky pass.

Of course, the backdrop of all that back-and-forth teasing only heightened the fun when Tilghman's forty-seven-yarder went through the uprights against Calvert Hall.

The Greyhounds went on to win by a score of 37–14.

Perhaps Biff should have added one more rule for the big homecoming dance.

No quacking.

Chapter Eighteen

AFTER ALMOST TWENTY YEARS OF SUPPORTING SICK children and their families—serving as a temporary home for more than thirty thousand families—the Baltimore Ronald McDonald House needed work. It needed money. So staff and volunteers organized a big fund-raising dinner in a hotel ballroom. More than eight hundred people showed up on a Saturday night, October 20, 2001, contributing $250 each for what was called the Spirit of Children Gala. Joe was the master of ceremonies.

"We have come to celebrate the strength and courage of children and their families who have faced diseases that have rocked the very foundations of their emotional and economic existence," Joe said in his opening remarks. "Yet they fight. These families fight every hour of every day for the healing and wholeness of their children."

Of course, Joe knew all too well what it was like to endure such drama. After an uplifting performance by the Maryland Children's Chorus, he silenced the room by telling the story of Billy Ehrmann. Most were hearing for the first time how Billy's death had forever changed the life of a fun-loving football star—and had led to Joe's role as co-founder of the Ronald McDonald House. But even for those who knew every detail, the story never got stale. In fact, it gained import through the years, as Joe and his community work, and therefore the memory of Billy, touched more and more people. Thirty thousand families at the

Ronald McDonald House alone! Thousands more at The Door. Countless others through Mission Baltimore and Building Men for Others.

Watching Joe speak in that hotel ballroom, enjoying the evening with my longtime girlfriend, Leslie Herpin, I thought quite a bit about Billy and his everlasting influence on his older brother. Joe often spoke in public about Billy. But what about the solitude that comes at the end of a day—how much did Joe still think about Billy when he was all alone with his thoughts? Did he ever wonder what his life would now be like, what he'd be doing, if Billy had never gotten sick? I wanted to ask Joe those questions. But this was a night for socializing, not probing. My curiosity could wait.

A few days later, I went to Joe's office for one of our talks. Our topic was the code of conduct he had created for any man built for others. First, though, I told Joe that I had a few questions about Billy.

"Okay," Joe said, leaning back in his usual chair across the table from me, wearing khakis and a short-sleeve pullover, arms folded across his chest.

"How often do you think about Billy?" I asked. "I know you always talk about him in public settings, but . . ."

"Oh, a lot," Joe said. "I think about him a lot."

He unfolded his arms and sat up. He brushed the fingertips of his right hand along the inside of his left forearm where, ever since the week of Billy's funeral, he had carried the tattooed words Head and Miss You along with a black dagger sticking through a red heart. "Head" was Billy's nickname, so large was his noggin. "Miss You" had double meaning: both the obvious longing for a loved one and the title of that favorite Rolling Stones song that Billy and Joe used to crank in the hospital.

"This tattoo has been a great blessing, like an anchor in my life," Joe said. "It's something I've always been able to touch, one of my greatest possessions, actually. But, yeah, I still think about him quite a bit. I think most of my passion has come out of that pain."

"Do you ever wonder what it would be like with Billy here?" I asked.

"Oh, yeah, all the time," Joe said.

"What are some of those thoughts that you have?"

"Well, he would probably be married and have kids. I've always wondered . . . what kind of man would he be? How close would we be? I'd like to think we'd be real close, but who knows? And I'm always amazed by thinking of him as a forty-two-year-old man. That's how I project and kind of play with that stuff."

"What about your own life?" I said. "How different would it be without that catalyst, that life-changing catalyst that you had?"

"I don't know . . . because I just see the hand of God. I don't know how to go back. I don't know how to take that apart. I just take it for what it is. And I've seen the tremendous amount of good that's come out of it."

Joe's code of conduct revolves around four "strategic masculinity traits" that form what he calls "the moral and ethical foundation" of a man built for others.

He accepts responsibility.

He leads courageously.

He enacts justice on behalf of others.

He expects God's greater rewards.

"That's a code of conduct that I think we have to teach,"

Joe said. "It will not just happen on its own. You have to be taught each of those four traits."

We took them one at a time.

"No matter what the circumstances, at some point in time you have to assume the wherewithal to take responsibility for the choices and decisions you make," Joe said. "You can't always slough that off and pass that on. So at first it's just teaching kids about things like being on time, doing their homework, showing up if they have a job. And certainly sports is a tremendous avenue to teach responsibility, because under the collective team responsibility, every individual has to be responsible for his own contribution and his own personal management of what he brings to the team."

Broadening the discussion beyond the Gilman boys, Joe touched on the "victim's mentality" that seemed to pop up more and more—being wielded as a crutch—throughout just about every segment of our society.

"Nobody grows up in a perfect family, simply does not exist, and we certainly don't live in a perfect society, so we find ourselves with an awful lot of nurturing wounds," Joe said. "And then what we get from that is a tendency to blame others or make an alibi for our own decisions and actions."

Joe offered an example: A father walks out on his wife and kids. The kids struggle without a male role model in the house. Then come the problems.

"But as a kid," Joe said, "even though your dad walked away, you've still eventually got to assume responsibility for yourself. And you've got to assume responsibility not to do that to *your* kids the next go-around."

"How do you get that point across to a boy when all he has seen is the father who walked out?" I asked.

"That's a long-term process," Joe said. "I think you have to help him understand and help him work through it. 'It's not so much what your father did, it's more that the responsibility is on what you do with that fact.' Everything in our culture teaches men to either deny or suppress or ignore this kind of pain. But we have to work through our own woundedness and whatever happened to us. We simply have to be responsible for what we do with the stuff that happens to us."

I thought of an old saying that a friend had shared with me years earlier: Life is only 10 percent what happens to us, 90 percent how we react to it.

On the subject of leadership, Joe said: "It's gotta be based on some kind of moral, ethical foundation. You can't just go with the flow in life. There's a broad road and a narrow road, and you have to learn how to courageously stand up on some kind of foundation, some kind of principle, make decisions, be a leader, and go that way. It takes great courage to lead in the right direction . . . and especially at the age of the boys on our football team. In the midst of all of the peer pressure, the whole social setting, it takes tremendous courage to stick to the right values because they're often gonna find themselves at odds with the rest of their peer group."

In other words, Joe said, they would be going against the flow.

He framed "the flow" as being all about the "I, me, mine" approach to life: "I'm at the center of the universe. 'You only go around once. Do it with *gusto*. Grab all you can.' Well, that flies in the face of all the stuff we want our boys to be about. So I think the courage to be different—to be a leader instead of just following the pack—has to be taught."

"How do you do that?" I asked. "How do you teach the courage to be a leader?"

"It has to be modeled," Joe said. "As a parent, I know my kids catch more of what they see me do than what they hear me tell them to do. That's for darn sure. So I think you build leadership in . . . and then you affirm it. Same way we create leadership on our football team."

"You say you *create* leadership—how do you do that?" I asked.

"By giving kids responsibility," Joe said. "You hold them accountable for that responsibility. And then you affirm them for making good on it. We try to teach all the kids on the team that they're leaders . . . because everybody's watching them. They're gonna make decisions, and when they make decisions, whether they're good or bad, other boys in the school are gonna go with them, just by the nature of the jersey that they wear, just because of the way that others look up to them as athletes."

"Big job for a kid," I said.

"Absolutely," Joe said. "But if you can do it as a high school football player, then we're also putting you on the right path to lead courageously as an adult."

Biff often spoke about the third strategic trait in Joe's code of conduct—enacting justice on behalf of others—in his chapel sessions at Gilman. Now I wanted to hear directly from Joe on the subject.

"The whole justice piece, it goes back to a basic concept of my masculinity or my humanity, because it is all about being other-centered," Joe said. "Woven all the way through this is a profound sense that you have to understand the pain of other people . . . and especially what causes it. When you see people suffering, I just think part of your responsibility is to *lead* in making sure that the pain is eradicated. That's a responsibility of every citizen in a community. You've got to figure out what's right or wrong. And then you have to act on that."

Joe said that justice should always be examined within the context of at least three broad categories: "It is relational, it is economic, and it is communal."

Relational: "You need justice in all relationships. Cheating on your wife or your girlfriend, not treating other people fairly, taking advantage of a situation that might benefit you but also hurts someone else in the process, that's all relationally unjust."

Economic: "Ever thinking that you can profit from some unjust gain, that's simply wrong. You've got to understand how that cuts away at the core of who you are and also understand the impact that it has on other people. Taking into consideration the impact on others—that is a moral absolute. And you've always got to maintain some sort of moral absolutes when it comes to economic right and wrong."

Communal: "Everybody ought to be able to participate in the community. When people are ostracized, when they're locked outside of the community for any number of reasons, you've got to do something about it. Just flat out *got* to. There's that old saying: 'You give a man a fish, and you feed him for a day. You teach him how to fish, and he can feed himself for a lifetime.' But if he can't even get to the pond, no matter how impressive his rod and reels are, what good are they? You gotta remove the barriers so the person can go fish. That's not only showing mercy. It's also a matter of justice."

I flipped through my notebook and found the page on

which I had written something I'd once heard Joe tell the Gilman boys. I read his words back to him: "Wherever there is injustice, we ought to show up, stand up, and *speak* up."

In response to hearing his own words—*wonderful string of words,* I thought—Joe said, "Whenever we can show up, stand up, and speak up, that's when we start changing the world . . . and all of us need to do that."

I had only seen the fourth trait of Joe's code of conduct listed in his Building Men for Others material. I had never really heard him talk about it—only tangentially—because he was generally reluctant to inject religious language into the secular environment at Gilman.

"Expects God's greater rewards," I said. "What do you mean by that?"

"I think there is a time when God is going to reward people that were relationally just and lived a life filled with cause," Joe said. "You don't need to 'get it all' in this world. You can say no to an awful lot of *things* so that you can be focused on other people. Ultimately, there is a day of reckoning. And that is for all eternity. You don't have to have the biggest house, the biggest car, all that kind of *stuff,* once you get there, and by knowing that, by expecting God's greater rewards, now you can free up your time and energy in this life to be about other people, to be about your causes."

"This one is quite different from the other three traits," I said. "This one is almost a motivation to encourage living by those other three."

"I've got so much stuff in this culture that's telling me to take care of my*self,*" Joe said. "I think in order for me to assume my responsibilities and to act courageously and to enact justice . . . I have to somehow stay focused on the fact that this ain't all there is, man. There is *some* design. There is *some* purpose in this world. And, ultimately, you're going to stand there and face up to that . . . for all eternity."

That somehow brought us all the way back to the first subject of our conversation. Billy Ehrmann.

"I do believe that we will eventually be reconnected," Joe said. "I've got a great longing there, but I know that it will be satisfied. I have total belief in that."

Joe glanced down at that tattoo on his forearm. Maybe he did it without even being aware that he looked. But I noticed.

Chapter Nineteen

THERE WAS NOTHING COMPLICATED ABOUT WHAT remained for the Gilman boys: two easy games against weak opponents and then the big season finale at McDonogh, heated rivals going head-to-head for the conference championship. Nobody would dare say it out loud, but the next two games were basically appetizers leading up to the main course against McDonogh. For now, all the Greyhounds wanted was to have some fun and stay healthy.

When the Gilman boys took the field at Loyola Blakefield—early afternoon the last Saturday in October—they were greeted by the first real chill of the season. The temperature was forty-four degrees and dark clouds filled the sky. Of course, Biff immediately declared it Gilman football weather. Joe went to the refreshment stand for a cup of coffee.

Perhaps the Gilman boys also should have sipped something warm to get themselves going against a team that had won only once in six games. The Greyhounds managed to score two touchdowns in the first half—Ambrose Wooden on a six-yard run in the first quarter and Napoleon Sykes on a ten-yard pass from Ambrose in the final minute of the second—but the failure of both extra-point attempts fit right in with a generally lackluster performance. Gilman led 12–0 at the half.

"We didn't bring all of our talents," Biff told the boys.

But he was not too concerned. After all, this was still

perennial powerhouse Gilman against a much smaller, slower, less talented team that had yet to exhibit any scoring power. The Gilman boys sat in one of the end zones and listened to individual critiques from their coaches. Then Napoleon stood up and appealed to his fellow starters—especially his senior classmates—to take charge early in the second half so that everyone else on the team would get plenty of playing time.

"We need to do this for the guys who have not played yet," Napoleon said.

A good number of the boys shouted back in full support of his message. But could passion just be flipped on like a light switch?

The second half began with an unfortunate thud. Malcolm Ruff, a key contributor at running back on offense and linebacker on defense, went down with a sprained ankle. He was done for the day . . . and whatever energy the Gilman boys had summoned up at halftime now seemed to be quickly lost. Nobody had much of an explanation for it, but the Greyhounds were simply flat. They dropped passes. They missed tackles. They blew assignments.

Meanwhile, the Loyola boys just kept plugging away, and with a major source of inspiration fueling their efforts. This was the final home game for their sixty-seven-year-old coach, Joe Brune, who was retiring after thirty-five seasons and more than two hundred victories. The Loyola Dons were not only seeking a major upset. They wanted to turn this into a going-away party.

Slowly but surely, Loyola chipped away. First came a short touchdown run by senior quarterback Marcus Frisby (Gilman blocked the point-after-touchdown kick). Next came a thirty-five-yard field goal that made the score way too close for comfort: Gilman 12, Loyola 9. That was the way it stayed into the fourth quarter. So much for Gilman making sure that its substitutes would get a lot of playing time. The Greyhounds were in a dogfight.

With less than three minutes left in the game, Frisby finished off a dramatic fifty-nine-yard drive with a short touchdown pass for Loyola's first lead of the day: 16–12. The place went wild. The Greyhounds still had time, but not much of it. They started at their own twenty-four-yard line with 2:37 left on the clock. The offense moved the ball well and was soon only twenty-nine yards from redemption in the Loyola end zone. But the defense made a stand. With forty-seven seconds to play, Gilman failed on a do-or-die, fourth-down pass. The ball went back to Loyola. Game over.

The scoreboard flashed a single word: AWESOME.

Fans rushed out of the stands and danced on the field.

The Loyola players swarmed Coach Brune and showered him with the contents of a large Gatorade bucket. Tears of joy streaked his cheeks. The departing coach could not have scripted a better ending.

Joe walked straight across the field to deliver a hug and a handshake.

"Congratulations," he told Brune. "I'm really happy for you."

Meanwhile, the Gilman boys stood dejected and confused. It was bad enough losing to top-notch teams like DeMatha, Urbana, and Poly Prep. But Loyola? It was almost inconceivable. The Greyhounds were once again mired in mediocrity—four wins, four losses—and with McDonogh only two weeks away.

With the sky now even darker than it had been a few hours earlier—or perhaps it only looked that way from the Gilman side of the field—the Greyhounds lined up to shake hands with the Loyola boys. But first Mike Dowling, eyes welling up, pacing like a wild animal, *stalking,* told his team-mates: "Remember this feeling. This is what it feels like when we don't come ready to play. Don't *ever* forget this!"

Once all the handshakes were done, Biff gathered his boys for final remarks before the bus ride back to Gilman.

"Let's give our opponents a lot of credit," he said. "They played their hearts out."

Shifting the focus to his own team, Biff said: "This has been a season where we've had a lot of bumps and bruises along the way. But I'm not disappointed in you. Not one bit. Our goal is still to win the league and beat McDonogh. Same exact thing we've been saying every day of every week. So here's where we stand. If we beat McDonogh, then we tie them for the best record in the league. And then the title really belongs to us . . . because we beat them. Look at me, boys."

Biff went into his less-is-more, whisper-for-emphasis mode.

"We've still got some breath left."

Raising the volume back to normal, he said: "What I care about is how you respond next week. Because then when something goes wrong later in your lives, that's the same way you'll respond then."

The Gilman boys were dead silent as their two yellow school buses pulled out of the Loyola parking lot. The final tally, 16–12, was still shining bright in red lights on the scoreboard. Perhaps that score would never really go away.

But not all was lost.

Sitting with Biff right behind the driver on the first bus, Joe eyeballed a huge plastic container of cookies and candy that one of the Gilman moms had left on the seat straight across the aisle from them. Joe secured an oversized choco-late chip cookie and started munching.

Biff did not eat anything. He just sat and stared into space. He stewed. The more he thought about what had happened on the field, the clearer it became. Forget what he had just told the boys. He *was* disappointed in them. Very disappointed. What in the world had they been doing out there? What had they been thinking about? Where was the senior leadership when everything headed south? Maybe he would address the boys one more time before they scattered for the rest of the weekend.

Biff did not tell anyone what he was thinking. In fact, when the buses emptied out back at Gilman, Joe went straight to his car and left without knowing he was about to miss a team meeting. The boys were getting out of their uniforms, packing away pads and helmets, when Biff unexpectedly entered their locker room. The look on his face made it perfectly clear that this was not going to be pleasant. If someone had dropped the proverbial pin to the floor, it would have landed with the reverberation of a train wreck in an echo chamber.

Biff told the boys that they were about to be out of the state rankings for the first time—not just knocked down a few spots, but eliminated. He also pointed out that the loss to Loyola was the first conference defeat Gilman had suffered in four years. It was not the losing that bothered Biff the most—nothing had changed the relative unimportance he attached to the outcome of any game. What really upset him was the attitude he had intermittently sensed throughout the season.

"Sometimes I just think we have a bunch of excuse makers on this team," Biff said. "Each time we lose, it gets easier to lose. We talk all the time about bringing your talents. You didn't bring 'em today. I'm extremely disappointed in you. I'm very disappointed in me too."

Biff went on for about ten minutes.

Once again, though, all was not lost. On his way out, Biff noticed that someone had relocated that big container of cookies and candy to a strategic spot on the floor of the locker room. He grabbed a couple of cookies for the ride home. Biff had been around long enough to know that high school boys—even the best of them—would at times test the patience of any man. But ruin his appetite for a tasty snack packed with sugar? Never. Biff would not allow it.

A week later—four hours before the penultimate game of the season—Biff walked to the front of the team meeting room and wrote an equation on the board.

Hope + Faith = Adversity + Despair Busters

It was his title for chapel before a two o'clock game at Dunbar High School.

"Hope and faith are the opposite of adversity and despair," Biff said. "And I think it is fairly appropriate we talk about that right now, because our season is kind of a microcosm of the way lives go sometimes. Sometimes you have very high expectations . . . you *must* have high expectations because you'll never accomplish anything without thinking that way, right? But sometimes things happen."

Biff gave a few examples: You might have a child get sick. You might be a doctor and lose a patient. Your business might fold. You might have the chance to do something really great to help somebody—and then not be able to get it done.

"But, look, it's never over until it's over," Biff said. "There's not a guy walking on the earth that hasn't had bad things happen to him . . . not a single guy who has not made gazillions of mistakes. That's not the issue. The issue is, what the heck do you do from there?"

In the big scheme of things, Biff reminded the boys, being four-and-four as a high school football team is pretty silly stuff compared to the adversity people face out in the real world. But hope and faith were just as important now, just as critical to the outcome of their season, as they always would be in confronting the adversity and despair of any given day.

The boys definitely got the message. At Dunbar, they erupted with five touchdowns in the first half and cruised to victory by the score of 42–0.

Early the next morning, the Greyhounds got together in a very different setting, this time to do something about real adversity and despair. They participated in a walkathon to support a program for the homeless. After that, the Gilman boys were officially ready to begin the last week of their season. McDonogh week.

Chapter Twenty

A LONG AND REVERED HISTORY ALWAYS SERVED AS motivational backdrop to McDonogh week. Gilman and McDonogh football teams had been going at each other since 1914. Any well-informed historian at either school would quickly be able to frame that year with three defining points: Woodrow Wilson was president. The first shots of World War I were fired. And the inaugural battle in what would become a major schoolboy rivalry ended in a blowout for the home team: Gilman 35, McDonogh 0.

Eighty-five times the Greyhounds and Eagles had clashed through the decades, with Gilman claiming fifty victories, McDonogh thirty, and five games ending in a tie. The most recent confrontation—the final game of the previous season—was a classic matchup. Gilman was riding a seventeen-game winning streak against Baltimore-area teams. McDonogh was undefeated on the season after nine games of its own. When all the hitting was done, the McDonogh Eagles stormed off Gilman's field with a 7–0 victory and temporary custodianship of the three-foot-high trophy—"our cup," Biff called it—for which the teams vie each year. For Gilman partisans, the most notable play of the game came in the second quarter, when McDonogh star Joe Benson—primarily known as a quarterback but also a defensive back—drilled Ambrose Wooden with a jarring blow after Ambrose had clearly crossed the sideline and was "safely" out of bounds. McDonogh was flagged for a late hit. But Gilman still got the worst of it. Ambrose was injured and missed the entire second half. The Gilman boys would never forget how they lost their star quarterback and then their winning streak as well—another memorable chapter added to the long lore of the rivalry.

For me, it seemed a bit ironic that I was now spending so much time with the Gilman football team, given my own extraordinary history with McDonogh. Twenty-seven years had passed since I first met Joe and the rest of the Baltimore Colts during their training camp at the school. But all I had to do was close my eyes and I could still see it all so vividly. The practice fields. The McDonogh football stadium. The back of the pickup truck on which I used to stand to pour Gatorade for the players as they walked from the fields to the locker room. That sign on the wall with my favorite poem—"That Guy in the Glass"—painted so meticulously in bold, blue letters.

With the Gilman season drawing to a close, I decided to share that poem with the Greyhounds. It seemed to be a good fit with Building Men for Others. And reading it to the boys would be a nice way to close a story I wanted to tell them . . . the whole background that explained why I, too, was getting pretty emotional about the upcoming visit to McDonogh. With that in mind, I found myself once again digging through the dresser drawer in which I had earlier found that old snapshot of Joe and the other keepsakes from my days with the Colts. It did not take me long to find the folded-up sheet of paper on which my eleven-year-old hand had carefully copied each line from that sign by the Colts locker room: "When you get what you want in your struggle for self and the world makes you king for a day . . ."

Maybe I should have stopped digging. But I saw a stack

of old mail stuffed away in a back corner of the drawer—
nothing to do with the Colts—and decided to take a look.

There were lots of cards and letters from my sister. I
guess that is one thing that happens when your only sister
and best friend—living clear across the country in San
Francisco—has already been saved by the miracle of organ
transplantation but still battles a deadly hepatitis B virus.
You tend to save whatever she sends you. Now thirty-four,
Wendy was enjoying a generous stretch of stable health. But
that did nothing to diminish something she had penned to
me years earlier: "You hold me steady through the stormiest
times. I don't know what I would do without you because I
love you so much."

There was also a letter from my brother, Jim, two years
older than me, a computer programmer in New York. Jim
and I had never been very close, which was precisely why
his letter meant so much to me. He had written it five years
earlier to thank me for being in his wedding party. The letter included the most expressive language I had ever seen
from my brother: "Thank you so much for being such a loving, supportive part of our life together. We love you very
much!"

I also found a beautiful letter from my mother, written
after I had been to Florida to celebrate her sixtieth birthday
with family and friends. Mom wrote: "Now I know I'm the
luckiest person in the world! I looked around me last weekend and felt so much love from the people who mean the
most to me. I've been telling everyone that those few days
were the very best in my 60 years on this earth. I truly feel
spoiled and love you so much."

No matter how many times I looked, there was still no
letter from my father in that drawer. I did find a 1991 newspaper story that included a picture of him teaching math at

his high school in New York. I had always been very proud
of the transition Dad had made at the age of fifty-five from
longtime actuary with a large insurance company to a new
career in teaching. It gave me great comfort to know how
happy he was in the classroom. But now I felt an emptiness
that might never be filled. I definitely would have traded
that yellowed newspaper clipping for a letter worthy of my
dresser drawer.

Gilman had a pep rally the day before the McDonogh
game. With the entire student body filling the stands over-
looking the football field, one of the highlights was a skit.
The plot centered on the fact that Gilman people had long
referred to McDonogh students as "the farmers" because
McDonogh had been founded, in 1873, as a farm school
for boys from poor families. With that in mind, Mike
Dowling and two of his schoolmates were dressed as farmers when they pulled up to the pep rally in an old Chevy
pickup. Mike wore overalls, a flannel shirt, work boots, and
a cowboy hat. The costumes alone elicited heckling from
the Gilman crowd. Then everyone saw that the uninvited
"farmers" had a prisoner tied up in the back of their truck.
It was Ambrose Wooden—and the farmers had even forced
the Gilman quarterback to wear a McDonogh T-shirt during
his captivity. Such horrid treatment! The Gilman faithful
were outraged! Ambrose was soon "rescued" by a band of
Gilman boys, and even Jon McGill, the Gilman headmaster, got in on the act. Wearing the Greyhound mascot's out-
fit, he liberated Ambrose from the McDonogh shirt and
ceremoniously cut it into shreds, much to the delight of the
Gilman boys. Their approval cascaded from the stands in
the form of cheers and laughter.

As much fun as Mike Dowling had playing such a prominent role in the pep rally, as much as he smiled and laughed, that whole day before his final high school football game was also a time of reflection and bittersweet emotions. Mike had so many great memories to take away with him. But there was also so much that he knew he would miss. One thing he hated to lose was the almost mystical feeling he sometimes got just being in the huddle with his teammates during a game.

"I love the huddle," Mike said. "There's such a strong feeling of co-dependency when you're all in there together. There's nothing like it in any other sport I've played. You don't have to pretend in the huddle. You don't have to cling to any false pretenses. Even the shape of it is perfect . . . a tightly wound circle. Everybody has their own ambitions and their own wants, but we all share the same desire too. You can just look in everyone's eyes and see that, and then once you realize how much everyone else wants it, that makes you want it even more."

In one sense, Saturday, November 10, 2001, was just like any other game day for the boys of Gilman. The schedule and rhythms were by now routine. But there was also a palpable feeling that this day was different. It was not only that the opponent was McDonogh. It was also the realization that something very special was coming to an end. This was the last day that the Gilman boys—this particular collection of boys—would ever spend together as a team.

"Okay, listen up," Biff said. "Championship number four. We're going after four in a row. And all of our goals, man, they're right here. Win the league and beat McDonogh. We're oh-and-oh. They're oh-and-oh. This is the Super Bowl, right? It's everything we've worked for. And, of course, I've been writing this on the practice schedule every day this week. Give us our cup back, all right? Just give us that daggone cup back. That thing doesn't belong at McDonogh. It belongs over here."

That was how Biff opened the chapel session. But he and Joe quickly went from rah-rah football talk to summary statements of a very different kind.

Joe paraphrased for the boys something the apostle Paul once wrote: "When I was a child, I did childish things. But when I became a man, I put away childish things."

Then Joe said: "You still want to have this childlike faith. You got to stop doing the childish *things* when you become a man, which is all the little pettiness, the comparing and competing with other people. But if you trust in and depend on some kind of spiritual power, then you can trust in and depend on the people next to you because you know that God is working through them as well. So you put away childish things as you become a man, but you still live with childlike faith and trust in both God and the people around you."

Joe stopped talking and sat down. The floor belonged to Biff.

"So now all you seniors start to put away childish things," he said. "I think you've learned some huge lessons about that this season."

Biff paused. Then he once again spoke directly to the boys who would soon suit up one final time in the blue and gray of the Gilman Greyhounds: "You seniors who are going away, I want to say something to you. You know, you don't *go* away. I don't like the word *go*. 'Go' kind of means you just leave, you're untethered, you break away from the moorings and just float around out there. Gilman football guys, we don't *go*. We're *sent*. Being sent has a whole different connotation. 'Sent' means you've got support. 'Sent' means you've got a home. 'Sent' means you have a purpose. 'Sent' means you can always come back. Being sent means people love you. It means you go out like a warrior because you've got something to do. And when you get it done, you come back to your home people because they're all there waiting for you. It's a sense of community and connectivity."

Biff told the boys that he routinely exchanged e-mails with former players who were off at college. He would expect to get e-mails from the departing seniors as well, and he promised that his responses would always be pretty much the same: "Glad to hear you're doing so well. Keep hitting the books. Do what's right. What have you done this week in service for others? Remember, you're built for others."

"That's it," Biff said. "You're getting that every week . . . same exact stuff. Because you're not going away. You're being sent."

Joe and Biff sat together on the lead bus to McDonogh. Joe read a newspaper. Biff picked at his fingernails. The Gilman boys were deep in thought, silent for the most part. As the bus turned up the drive to McDonogh—a sprawling campus now awash in the school colors of orange and black—Biff said: "Man, I wish I could put on the pads today." Joe smiled but said nothing in return. He certainly did not share Biff's desire.

I walked with Joe from the bus to the football stadium, savoring every step in my stroll down memory lane. When I saw the track around the football field, it reminded me that the first coach I had ever known with the Colts, Howard Schnellenberger, still owed me a dollar from a bet I won as an eleven-year-old by beating one of his players in a race. So what if defensive back Brian Herosian let me win? That did not stop me from wondering how much that dollar, with twenty-seven years of compounded interest, would be worth now. Joe and I laughed about that. I also enjoyed seeing the hill by the old football practice fields on the other side of the tennis courts—the hill on which Joe and I were sitting when he first tagged me "Brillo." Being back at McDonogh somehow made me feel both young and old at the same time.

Once pre-game stretching and drills were done, the Greyhounds gathered under the stands for final remarks.

"That was the best warmup we've had all year," Biff told the boys.

"Maybe ever," Joe said.

"We are as good today as we have ever been," Biff said. "*Ever*. We're *better* today than we've ever been."

It was quite a declaration from a coach whose teams had ended two of the four previous seasons undefeated and on top of the state rankings. Gilman now had a record of five wins and four losses. McDonogh was a perfect nine-and-oh. Riding a two-year, nineteen-game winning streak, the Eagles were the number-one team in Baltimore.

"I don't want to see any talking to the other team," Biff said. "No talking trash. No woofing. No pushing. No nothing. Just bring the fire. They have not been where we've been. They have not played the kind of teams we've played. This will be the sweetest victory for us since we've been here."

Ambrose Wooden was last to speak in a players-only huddle just before the start of the game: "Seniors, we've been together through thick and thin. This is our last time together. Let's do it!"

The Greyhounds shouted back in rowdy agreement.

They also responded very well on the field. In a remarkable opening drive defined by both well-executed offense that pushed the Greyhounds forward and frustrating penalties that moved them back, Gilman consumed almost the entire first quarter while running nineteen plays and marching eighty yards for the first score (a twenty-yard touchdown pass from Ambrose to Anthony Triplin). When McDonogh fumbled on its first offensive play, Gilman immediately reclaimed possession with only fourteen yards to go for another score. Seven plays later, Malcolm Ruff punched the ball into the end zone on a two-yard run early in the second quarter, and just like that, Gilman was off to a 14–0 lead before McDonogh could do anything at all. The home crowd was stunned into silence.

"Hey," Biff shouted on the Gilman sideline, "we're here to take our cup back."

There was no more scoring in the second quarter.

Once again gathered under the stands at halftime, the Gilman boys were as fired up as they had been all season.

Joe felt obliged to remind them of what had happened two weeks earlier at Loyola—that total collapse in the second half. "Not to put a damper on anything," he said, "but this thing is far from over, right? Don't think McDonogh is done. They're coming back for more. And we don't want to have any regrets after this game."

Sending the boys out for the second half, Biff told them one last thing: "This is a reward for the strength of our schedule. You enjoy the heck out of these last twenty-four minutes."

Not so fast, the McDonogh boys said with their intensity in the third quarter. First the Eagles stopped the Greyhounds on a fourth-and-one quarterback keeper at the McDonogh thirty-three-yard line. Then the boys in orange jerseys drove down the field and finally got on the scoreboard after a Houdini-like escape by quarterback Joe Benson. With blitzing linebacker David Caperna wrapped around his legs and defensive lineman Luke Wilson grabbing at his upper body, Benson, facing the wrong end of the field, somehow spun around and lobbed a pass toward the back of the end zone. Wide receiver Eddie Dolch came down with it—a three-yard touchdown pass that actually floated about twenty-five yards through the air after Benson had taken a deep drop and been chased even farther away from the line of scrimmage. When the extra point sailed through the uprights, Gilman's lead was down to 14–7 with 5:25 left in the quarter.

With both offenses squandering chances and both defenses making big plays at all the crucial moments—including a gutty goal-line stand by Gilman—the score stayed that way deep into the fourth quarter. The Greyhounds were in great shape as they crossed midfield into McDonogh territory with about seven minutes left in the game. But then Ambrose fumbled a snap from center and the Eagles regained possession at their own forty-eight-yard line. Eight plays later, Benson threw an eight-yard touchdown pass, and with only 2:31 to play, the score was tied at 14. Nobody wanted the game to end that way. But McDonogh would at least secure the league title with a tie. Gilman needed a victory.

Such an outcome looked just about impossible when Ambrose overthrew tight end Stan White and McDonogh intercepted the ball at its own forty-four-yard line. With 1:58 left, the McDonogh players and fans sensed the makings of an amazing come-from-behind victory. But then came another shocker. McDonogh fumbled—and Gilman got the ball right back! This was not only a football game. It was also a cardiology exam.

The final stress test started at Gilman's forty-eight-yard line with 1:11 left in the game. A holding penalty sent the Greyhounds back to their thirty-five. But then Ambrose made a nice run back to the original line of scrimmage. From there, he went to his most prolific receiver, Stan White, who caught the ball for a twenty-eight-yard gain and a first down at the McDonogh twenty-four. Sixteen seconds remained. Ambrose went right back to Stan, who hauled in a short pass and went out of bounds at the twenty-yard line. Nine seconds showed on the scoreboard clock. Everyone knew the math: seven yards back from the line of scrimmage for the placement of the ball, ten more yards through the end zone to the goal posts. It would be a thirty-seven-yard field goal attempt. Biff called for his kicker.

With eighty-seven years of Gilman-McDonogh football history looming over the stadium, invisible to the eye but nonetheless weighing on the hearts and minds of all, the whole season came down to this: one play, one swift stroke of boot against ball, either a shining moment that would last a lifetime or—no, please, no—a twin horror to match the agony Tilghman Morton had suffered a year earlier when that dying duck of a kick had missed the mark against State College.

If a screenwriter had the audacity to make it up this way for the closing scene of a movie, he would deserve to be laughed right out of Hollywood. *Yeah, right, and as long as we're going totally cliché, why don't we also make it so this Tilghman kid is playing hurt?*

Actually, Tilghman *was* nursing an injury, a strained hip flexor he had aggravated just two days earlier in practice. Fortunately, Tilghman kicked with his left foot and the problem was on the opposite side. But what about his ability to plant his right foot properly and thereby be able to generate the power he would need to send that football through the uprights? After limping around school the day before, Tilghman had taken ibuprofen to fight the swelling. But he had still been tentative during pre-game warmups. It was only at the last minute that Gilman trainer Lori Bristow had cleared him to play.

As if the plot were not already thick enough, there was also the family wedding. Tilghman's thirty-one-year-old sister, Caroline, was getting married three and a half hours later in Washington. That meant that Tilghman's dad was about to miss the biggest moment—best or worst—of his only son's high school sports career. John Morton, a prominent bank executive and chairman of a blue-ribbon committee trying to lure the 2012 Olympics to the region, did not take such a moment lightly. He had not missed a Gilman game all season. In fact, he was usually in the stands an hour before kickoff to set up his video equipment and watch the Greyhounds warm up. As father of the bride, though, he was without any choice. He had left the football game during the third quarter. But he was still following the action as best he could. While Tilghman trotted onto the field to win or lose the conference championship, John Morton drove south on Interstate 95 with a cell phone pressed to his left ear. A friend, John Claster, was reporting to him from the stands at McDonogh.

"Tilghman's on the field," Claster said. Then he held his phone up in the air.

John Morton listened to the Gilman fans chanting encouragement—"Tilgh-man, Tilgh-man"—and he could hardly believe the whole situation. It was almost surreal to him.

Tilghman tried to ignore the crowd. But how could he? Though nervous about the kick, he also felt so proud to have all those people behind him.

McDonogh called for a timeout.

Good, Tilghman thought. *Plenty of time to get yourself together.* He visualized his kicking mechanics, then he literally walked through his steps one last time.

"No problem," said Napoleon Sykes, who would hold the ball for Tilghman. "Just kick it. Same as always."

The two of them being together for this dramatic climax to the season—holder and kicker working as one—was in a sense poetic perfection. Just as Ambrose Wooden and Mike Dowling had so neatly represented the whole concept of Building Men for Others during that poignant exchange after the game at Urbana—relationships before anything else—so too did Napoleon and Tilghman stand together as ideal symbols of the program. The son of a city bus driver teaming up with the son of a well-to-do bank president . . . each needing the other . . . each there for the other. Perfection.

The referee finally blew his whistle to initiate play. On both sides of the ball, boys dug in with equal parts excitement and trepidation.

Tilghman put his head down and locked his eyes on the spot that he and Napoleon had selected for the placement of the football. Sophomore center Drum Rice snapped the ball through his legs and Napoleon snatched it out of the air. He quickly but carefully steadied its nose on the chosen ground. And then . . . *bam* . . . Tilghman tore through that ball with all his might. A jolt of pain shot through his right side, but that was only temporary. The outcome of this play would last forever. The kick was low, nothing pretty, but it triggered the most beautiful sight in the world. With only one second left on the clock, the referee raised his arms to signal that the field goal was good!

Yes!

The Gilman boys and their fans erupted in sheer ecstasy.

The roar of the crowd was all John Morton needed to hear. Alone behind the wheel of his Suburban, still on the interstate but also in a bit of a fog, tears of joy and relief rolled down his cheeks. He was lucky not to plow into an eighteen-wheeler.

Meanwhile, the football field was transformed into a canvas of contrasts. The boys of McDonogh were frozen in disbelief and disappointment. The boys of Gilman jumped up and down, pumped fists in the air, unleashed shouts of glee, squeezed one another in tight hugs. This time it was Biff who was showered with the contents of a Gatorade bucket. One of the assistant coaches, Keith Kormanik, handed out white T-shirts with blue lettering. On the front: "We Have Waited A Year." On the back: "Now Give Us Back Our Cup."

In the middle of all the madness, Joe put his head down and crossed the field to shake hands with the McDonogh coaches. Joe posed for pictures with a few of his players, but only when asked to do so. Otherwise, he stood back from the vortex of the celebration, chatting calmly with Gilman parents and friends.

Eventually, Biff gathered the boys in one spot and settled them down—at least temporarily—so that he could share a few thoughts.

"What an unbelievable season," he said. "Fourth championship in five years. And this is the sweetest of all. It's tough to start out oh-and-two in anything—sports, business, life. But we stayed together. Everything we did, we did it together. And I'll guarantee you, you will never forget this day for as long as you live."

The on-field frolicking started up again when Biff was

done speaking. Clearly, the Gilman boys did not want to let go of what they were feeling.

Mike Dowling was the only exception. Though immeasurably thrilled by the game itself, he was also overcome by sadness. He could not shake the stinging disappointment—the emptiness—of knowing that his father had not bothered to show up for his final high school football game.

"Didn't even come to my last game," Mike told Biff through tears.

"I'll stand in for your dad today," Biff said.

When they hugged, Mike rested his head on Biff's left shoulder and wept.

Soon thereafter, Tilghman Morton, still in his football pants and the soiled T-shirt he had worn under his shoulder pads, walked into the lobby of the Willard Hotel in downtown Washington. The rest of his family was just leaving for pre-wedding pictures.

"I'm so proud of you," John Morton said to his son.

Tilghman would later tell me, "It made me feel so special just to hear him tell me that. I hated that I had to rush away from McDonogh and not be with everyone else for the big celebration. But going from the game to the wedding, seeing my dad so happy and proud, I think it was the greatest day of my life."

After forty-five minutes of post-game celebration and general lingering in the warm afterglow of Greyhound glory, Joe and Biff finally ushered the last of the Gilman boys off the field.

Walking to their buses, Biff turned to Joe and said, "Best season yet, huh?"

"Kids learned a lot of stuff this year," Joe said.

The buses were parked next to the old field house that once served as the summer home of the Baltimore Colts. As we approached, the late-afternoon sun was setting into the woods behind the building, melting slowly into treetops. I took one last look back at that hill where I had long before become Brillo; took one final glance up at the soft, fading sun; and that was when the thought first crystallized for me. Like the Gilman boys, I was not really going away. I was being sent.

Chapter Twenty-one

IN THE SILENCE OF MY MIND, I COULD NOT ESCAPE THE simple but powerful philosophy of my first high school basketball coach: "No regrets." I heard those words as I drove home after the last Gilman game. I heard them while lying in bed that night. I heard them the next few days as I pondered the potential ramifications of what I seemed to be on the verge of doing, then weighed those possible outcomes against the cost of not doing anything at all. Ultimately, the power of those two words—a guiding force that had always served me well—finally convinced me that I really had no choice. I had to take action.

My season with Joe had forced me to explore a multitude of thoughts about my dad. Now I had to do something in response to all that thinking. I needed to look into my father's eyes and start a dialogue about our relationship. So I made plans to visit him in New York. I was not going away. I was being sent.

This was a daunting proposition. What exactly would I say to my unsuspecting dad? How would I make myself clear without hurting the one man I loved more than any other man in the world? Or would it even be possible to articulate what I needed to say without bruising him?

All I told my dad on the phone was that I wanted to spend an evening with him, just the two of us, so that I could talk to him about the whole experience I had just been through with Joe, Biff, and the Gilman boys.

"Great," Dad said. "I'm glad you're coming."

If only he knew, I thought. *Oh, man, if only he knew.*

Ten days after the Gilman-McDonogh game—early the Tuesday morning before Thanksgiving—I reached down into the pile in the back corner of my office for that book Joe had given me. I once again read *Questions for My Father,* taking notes this time, and then I put the book in my travel bag for the drive to New York. Being out on the road some- how diminished the apprehension I'd been battling in anticipation of the conversation I would soon initiate. Maybe it was a matter of being relieved that I was finally acting on thoughts that had percolated for months. Whatever the reason, my anxiety slowly went away, and I began to feel eager about sitting down with my dad. I kept telling myself that this would be the unanticipated payoff of my whole unexpected journey with Joe. This would be the pot-of-gold destination I had never sought but had some- how found.

It was early evening when I pulled into the driveway of my dad's house in Bedford, New York, a bucolic suburb about an hour north of New York City. I was excited just to see Dad and his wife, Leslie, because almost half a year had slipped away since we'd last been together. When my dad stepped outside to greet me, I pretty much saw myself, only a smaller and older version. We were often told how much we looked like each other: same shiny, bald domes framed by short hair on the sides and in the back; same big noses claiming control of our profiles; same easy, disarming smiles stretching the corners of our mouths and lighting up our brown eyes.

"Hey, Dad."

"You made it."

We shook hands and I patted my father on the shoulder. I knew not to go for a hug. Dad was not a hugger—not with another man. Of course, Leslie did not hesitate to give me both a hug and a kiss.

The three of us went to dinner at a casual Italian restaurant. Dad and I covered the same topics of conversation that we usually shared: family updates, his teaching, my writing, the stock market. Then we returned to the house. Leslie knowingly excused herself and went upstairs. Dad and I settled on a couch in the den. It was time for our big talk.

I started with some background about Joe and his definition of masculinity, stressing how he always put the emphasis on relationships before anything else. I explained how my conversations with Joe had repeatedly triggered thoughts about our own father-son relationship, how those thoughts had been with me for months now, how I could not go any longer without sharing them with him.

"I think some of this stuff has been bubbling below the surface for years," I said. "But this whole journey with Joe has served as a catalyst."

Not that this was going to be easy. I struggled with my words. I shifted forward and back on the couch.

"Uh, I'm gonna ramble here a little bit," I said.

I went through the whole thing about the six guys I considered my closest male friends—how four had already lost their fathers and the other two had long struggled in dysfunctional relationships with their dads.

"Wow," my father said.

"Yeah, well, I'm just saying, I come from a starting point where I feel incredibly fortunate, and always have," I said. "I have nothing but great things to look back on as far as being a child and my thoughts about you being my father. I mean, that's all extremely positive stuff. *But . . . "* I took a deep breath and quickly exhaled with audible force. "Having said that, there's still something missing, a certain openness or directness or whatever the right word is. We don't have any problem talking. It's more a matter of *what* we talk about, the things we share and things we don't. I guess it's really about the ability—or *in*ability—to express feelings and emotions. I mean, this probably sounds kind of strange for a son to say to his father, and it's not an easy thing for me to say, but sometimes I feel like we don't really know each other as well as we should."

My words hung in the air without any response. But I had to believe, certainly *wanted* to believe, that Dad was absorbing and processing everything I said. He had always been a very good listener, one of the best I'd ever known.

I tried a new tack, something to accentuate the positive: "If you look at the total time we have together in this world in, say, thirds—a third where I was a child, a third so far as an adult, maybe a third to go—this is an opportunity to start talking about some things and just make whatever time is left the greatest. I just want to make our connection the best it can be. Period."

Again, I stressed, it was not that I felt we had a *bad* relationship.

"I understand what you're saying," Dad said. "It can go beyond what it is."

"Exactly," I said. "It's a longing for something more. It's a very natural thing to want. And it's a huge *gift* that we even have the chance to talk like this. I'm not saying that things are just gonna all of a sudden change. But they'll never go anywhere if we don't at least start."

I glanced at a page of notes I'd scribbled on my way to New York.

"Two little things I thought of while I was driving up today," I said. "I was trying to think of examples that illustrate or symbolize the broad scope of the stuff I'm talking about. The first one is hugging. I know a lot of this is just our own emotional makeup, or our own background, or whatever goes into these things, but I think of the fact that the few times I've ever gone to hug you, that's not a comfortable thing for you. You shy away from that. I want to be able . . ."

My voice got stuck right there—just got caught for a moment—but I looked straight into my dad's eyes and continued as best I could: "If I want to hug you, I want to be able to hug you. It's not like I'm some little kid that always needs that, but that's just something I want to do sometimes. I don't want to ever have you leave this world and have me back here thinking I couldn't hug my dad when I wanted to."

The second example involved my girlfriend. I knew that Dad cared about whatever I was doing with my Leslie—we'd been together for two years—but why would he question my sister about where the relationship might be headed instead of just asking me directly?

"If you want to know something like that, want to know *any*thing, I want you to ask me," I said. "Because, number one, it makes me feel bad if you don't feel comfortable enough with me to ask me something like that. It makes me wonder what kind of son I am if you can't ask me. But it also makes me feel bad, like, What's going on with *you* that you can't ask me that? Does that make sense?"

"It does," Dad answered quietly.

"And, again, that's not being critical. It's just a matter of wanting more than that. I want better than that—for both of us."

———

I explained how Joe often used that signature line from the Lone Ranger—how so many sons lose their fathers and are then forever haunted by the question: Who was that masked man? I said that we could not allow that to happen. I could never live with that.

I showed Dad the little book, *Questions for My Father,* that I'd brought with me. I told him the background and said that maybe we could use some of the questions to help us start talking about things we'd never discussed.

Ever the schoolteacher—and also someone who liked to ease the tension of an uncomfortable situation by making light of it—Dad joked that maybe we ought to start with the multiple-choice questions.

"There's no multiple choice, Dad."

But we also had no ground rules. He could just pass on any question. He could *ask* anything he wanted to ask. We could bounce around and take off on any tangents that came to mind. The questions from the book were only a starting point.

"Fire away," Dad said.

And so I did. For almost three hours, I asked questions from the book and questions of my own. We talked about my dad's childhood. I learned that one of his fondest memories of being a little boy was going with his father to a railroad yard on Long Island. He loved watching the trains. We discussed Dad's college years and his time in the Navy. I'd always known that he had served a few years as an officer in return for the Navy's ROTC scholarship that put him through the University of Pennsylvania, but this was the first time I heard specifics about assignments that took him on an ammunition ship to Lebanon, Italy, Spain, and France. We talked about marriage and divorce, fatherhood and friendship, motivation and philosophy, politics and religion, life and death. We covered all sorts of ground we had always either tiptoed around or avoided altogether. When we were done, just before midnight, I knew Richard Marx better than I'd ever known him.

"I'm glad you brought all this up," Dad said.

"Me too."

Now it was his turn to ask a question: "So where do we go from here? How do we work on this? Because I want to. I really want to."

"Don't really know," I said. "But I think a lot will happen now just because it's all out on the table."

We got up from the couch.

"So you gonna let me hug you, Dad?"

He did not really answer. I just moved toward him and did it. I hugged more than he did, but I unmistakably felt his arms draped loosely around my lower back. It was nice to have them there.

"You're smothering me," my dad protested.

But he was smiling. I think he actually liked it.

The Monday morning after Thanksgiving, I finally did something that I had talked about for years but had never made the time to do. I went to school with my dad and watched him teach. We were both excited about it. I watched Dad teach algebra and geometry. He was relaxed and patient with his students, and he managed to keep them engaged even when the subject matter—square roots in one class—was not exactly scintillating. Seeing him in action made me proud.

I was driving straight back that day from the school in New York to my home in Washington. But first I left a note where my dad would later find it on his desk in the faculty room: "You are the best teacher I've ever known. Please know how thankful I am that I have always been one of your students—and that now I've even been to your classes. Love always, Jeff."

Over the next few weeks, both the frequency and quality of our telephone conversations picked up considerably. My father even surprised me one night with something he'd been thinking about: He wanted to visit me for a weekend. It had been several years since Dad had visited unless he was already coming to town for another reason. But now everything was different. He was intentionally reaching out to me. And I was immeasurably grateful for that.

We ended up having a wonderful weekend together— visiting museums, walking around Georgetown, just talking a lot. It didn't really matter *what* we did. Just being together was all I cared about.

Dad clearly felt the same way. When we said goodbye, it was he who made the first move toward a hug, and this time he held on and squeezed just as much as I did.

"I love you," he said.

"I love you, Dad."